A-LEVEL

STUDENT GUIDE

Ella Hansford

WJEC

History

Unit 5: Historical interpretations (non-examination assessment)

Phil Star

HODDER
EDUCATION
AN HACHETTE UK COMPANY

Hodder Education, an Hachette UK company, Blenheim Court, George Street, Banbury, Oxfordshire OX16 5BH

Orders

Bookpoint Ltd, 130 Milton Park, Abingdon, Oxfordshire OX14 4SB

tel: 01235 827720

fax: 01235 400401

e-mail: education@bookpoint.co.uk

Lines are open 9.00 a.m.–5.00 p.m., Monday to Saturday, with a 24-hour message answering service. You can also order through the Hodder Education website: www.hoddereducation.co.uk

ISBN 978-1-5104-5146-9

First printed 2019

Impression number 5 4 3 2 1

Year 2023 2022 2021 2020 2019

Cover photo: zhu difeng/Adobe Stock. Other photographs: World History Archive/Alamy Stock Photo (p.41); TopFoto.co.uk (p.71)

Typeset by Integra Software Services Pvt. Ltd., Pondicherry, India

Printed in Dubai

Hachette UK's policy is to use papers that are natural, renewable and recyclable products and made from wood grown in well-managed forests and other controlled sources. The logging and manufacturing processes are expected to conform to the environmental regulations of the country of origin.

Contents

Getting the most from this book 4

Content Guidance

What is the NEA? 5

Topics and questions 6

How is your essay assessed? 9

Working independently 13

Defining source material 15

Planning and structuring your essay 18

Carrying out research for your essay 21

Setting out an introduction 24

Historical interpretations and the developing
historical debate 27

Analysing and evaluating primary source material
for the NEA 37

From draft to finished product 50

Reviewing your work — formal and specific 56

A completed example 61

Applying the checklist 73

Submitting your essay 74

Appendix 1 Mark scheme 75

Appendix 2 Self-assessment grids 77

Index 79

■ Getting the most from this book

Tip

Advice on key points to help you organise, research and complete your NEA assignment in order to boost your grade.
....

Summaries

■ Each core topic is rounded off by a bullet-list summary for quick-check reference of what you need to know.

■ A completed example

Here is an example of a completed NEA. It includes some examiner comments to demonstrate the extent to which the essay fulfils the assessment criteria.

Historians disagree about the reasons why the Civil Rights movement was a success. How far do you agree that the main reason why the Civil Rights movement was a success in the 1960s was the leadership of Martin Luther King?

Exam-style questions

The question gives the opportunity to offer a substantiated judgement — note the use of the phrase 'the main reason' — and invites analysis of a major historical debate — the reasons for the success of the Civil Rights movement in the 1960s.

Martin Luther King was instrumental in the success of the Civil Rights movement. His peaceful protests and powerful speeches gained mass publicity worldwide and his belief in non-violent methods to achieve equality came from what he saw of Gandhi and what he did over the British Empire. King's role was hugely significant for the African-American equality movement from the acts of the Bus Boycotts in the mid-1950s until his death in 1968. His Nobel Prize award in 1964 came from his influential speeches such as the March to Washington the previous year and the passing of the Voting Act and Civil Rights Act while Johnson was President.

There is a hint of an answer in the first sentence but it could be much more focused on the actual question. Note the drift away from 'success' to 'significance'. They are linked but they are not the same historical concepts.

Sample student answers

While King was massively important in the Civil Rights movement and is considered the main reason for the success by historians, there are many other factors that have to be taken into account for the many victories that were gained by other key figures. This essay will argue against the question of King's leadership being the main reason for success in the Civil Rights movement. Lyndon B. Johnson, Malcolm X and many other groups have to be taken into account for their great work that helped black Americans achieve equality when there was nothing. Laws were passed and respect was gained due to the impressive work that they put in during the 1960s.

This is a more focused paragraph which attempts to give an answer 'in a nutshell'. There is a reference to 'historians' which hopefully will set up the opportunity to look at the developing historical debate about the success of the Civil Rights movement in the 1960s.

In the summer of 1963, 200,000 men and women gathered in Washington to listen to a man who is widely considered the most significant factor of the Civil Rights movement. On 28 August he made his 'I have a dream' speech which brought worldwide attention to Martin Luther King himself and also the violence and injustice on black Americans through the media.

Unit 5: Historical interpretations (non-examination assessment) 61

Content Guidance

■ What is the NEA?

WJEC History at A-level is assessed through five units. Four of these units are assessed by formally timed, written examinations — Unit 1 (a Period Study); Units 2 and 4 (connected Depth Studies); and Unit 3 (a Breadth Study). These units are examined and assessed by WJEC external examiners.

The fifth unit, the Non-Examination Assessment (NEA), is different. The NEA is your opportunity to produce an independent piece of work in relation to a question on an issue of historical debate. The basic stages are as follows:

- The question that you choose to answer is agreed after negotiation with your teacher.
- Your answer to the question is completed.
- Your answer is assessed internally by your teacher.
- Your answer is moderated by WJEC.

The NEA is worth 20% of the total A-level marks and is equivalent in value to each of the four written examinations. It is completed in Year 13 in most examination centres in Wales. You have to complete an essay of up to 4,000 words, which discusses different interpretations of an issue that has generated considerable historical debate.

The NEA is essentially an investigation into and evaluation of an issue that is open to a number of different historical interpretations. You will be required to demonstrate historical knowledge of the issue or development under debate and to show that you understand why different historical interpretations have been made of those issues or developments. You will also be given the opportunity to show an understanding of the method and work of historians.

In the Non-Examination Assessment you will need to:

- consider the developing historical debate about the issue set in the question by discussing at least two differing or contrasting historical interpretations
- research and be aware of the work of at least two historians and their interpretations

> **Tip**
>
> Discussion of the developing historical debate does not mean listing historians and their interpretations. It involves studying the reasons why such interpretations have developed.

> **Tip**
>
> Don't exceed 4,000 words. This would not fulfil the criteria for Band 6, which insist on a response that is 'coherent, lucid, concise and well-constructed'. A range of 3,300–3,800 words is ideal.

> **Tip**
>
> 'Interpretations' are judgements made by historians on historical events and developments.

Sometimes the developing historical debate is defined as 'historiography'. Sometimes 'historiography' is taken to mean outlining or relaying the views of a number of historians. However, this is not really what is required in your NEA. In your NEA you are expected to discuss the reasons which have encouraged the development of the historical debate regarding the set issue. This involves evaluating the historians' interpretations by understanding the context in which they were made.

Another key part of your NEA work is that you will need to research and select a range of primary and contemporary source material. You need to discuss how and why this evidence from your range of selected sources may be of value to historians forming differing, contrasting or alternative interpretations. This goes beyond stating that 'this source is of value to X because…'.

Your NEA requires you to use the source evaluation skills you have developed throughout your study of history to show an understanding of how historians would consider a range of primary and/or contemporary evidence in making an interpretation.

Tip

The NEA allows you to show an understanding of how the range of primary and/or contemporary evidence can be used to support different or contrasting interpretations.

Summary

- The NEA allows you to use and demonstrate the skills you have already developed in your study of history.
- You are given the opportunity to investigate, debate and come to a judgement on the issue set in your question.
- You will need to research and evaluate primary sources of information.
- You will need to discuss how the historical debate has developed over the set issue.

■ Topics and questions

The choice of topic and question for the NEA is very wide. In order to ensure that the questions set for NEA are appropriate and consistent in what they demand of students, all questions are approved in advance by WJEC senior moderators. Approval must be sought by a teacher in your school or college.

When it comes to setting a question for your NEA, there are two possibilities. Either your teacher will propose a question after discussion with you, or you will get the opportunity to choose one yourself.

The question that you propose should offer you the chance to achieve one or more of the following:

- extend and enhance your knowledge of aspects of the history studied in the broader units of the course
- study a topic that extends or changes the range or scale of your historical knowledge
- study an issue over a longer time period, such as several decades
- study a different type of history, such as local or regional history
- complement learning in other areas of your studies, including the opportunities provided in your other subjects

Choosing an appropriate NEA question

Whether you are choosing a question offered by your centre or choosing your own distinct question, there are a number of points to consider to make sure that your question gets WJEC approval.

The appropriateness of your question will be judged on:

- whether the topic is a recognisable or mainstream issue — it must not be too obscure
- whether there is a clear historical debate over the issue set in the question
- whether the question contains an evaluative term or statement that enables a valid and supported judgement to be reached
- whether there is a sufficient range of primary or contemporary material to allow you to evaluate the evidence base that enables historians to make their varying interpretations

Unless these aspects are present, it will be impossible for you to address all the assessment objectives (AOs) effectively and your question(s) will not be approved.

There is one other important rule to remember when choosing your question. To avoid narrowness of coverage over the GCE History course as a whole, the topic and question chosen for your NEA cannot come from the content specified in the Depth Study that you are studying for Units 2 and 4. For example, if your centre has chosen to teach the Depth Study on the Mid Tudor Crisis for Units 2 and 4, it would not be possible to set a question on different interpretations of the dissolution of the monasteries. This would mean that 60% of the coverage and assessment of the whole GCE course was on a very narrow historical period.

You can, however, revisit topics from the taught Period Study or Breadth Study in more depth, or consider topics from the history of anywhere else in the world, as long as there are enough primary sources and differing interpretations to allow you to engage with the debate over the issue.

Although the NEA cannot be based on the Depth Study, it can be based on the same years studied in the Depth Study. For example, learners studying Nazi Germany 1933–45 in Unit 4 could look at the policy of appeasement in the late 1930s from a British perspective or the Depression in the USA during the 1930s.

Tip

An evaluative term or statement allows a debate over the issue to take place and a valid judgement to be reached. Examples of evaluative terms are words such as 'mainly', 'mostly' and 'largely'. Evaluative statements include phrases such as 'to what extent' and 'how valid'.

Task 1

Would these questions be approved for the NEA?

The following checklist summarises the requirements for an NEA question:

- Is the topic a recognisable or mainstream issue?
- Is there a clear historical debate over the issue set in the question?
- Does the question use an evaluative term that enables such a debate to be engaged with?
- Is there a sufficient range of primary source material to allow a student to evaluate the evidence base that enables historians to make their varying interpretations?

Consider the following questions alongside the checklist. Do they fulfil the requirements?

- 'Chamberlain deserves to be judged as a guilty man for his policy of appeasement towards Germany 1937–39.' How valid is this assessment of Chamberlain's foreign policy up to the declaration of war in September 1939?
- How far do you agree that the bombing of Hiroshima and Nagasaki was aimed at intimidating the USSR?
- 'The German bid for continental supremacy was mainly responsible for bringing about a European war by 1914.' How valid is this assessment of the reasons for the increase in tension in Europe between 1878 and 1914?
- 'The Reichstag Fire was a deliberate attempt hatched by the Nazis to consolidate their control over Germany in 1933.' How valid is this assessment of the Reichstag Fire?
- Historians disagree about the role of Owain Glyndwr. How far do you agree that Owain Glyndwr was primarily a rebel and a murderer in the period 1400–15?
- 'The WSPU hindered the campaign for women's suffrage.' How valid is this assessment of the impact of the WSPU between 1906 and 1918?
- 'The Vikings were just the priest-slaying bogeymen of the early Middle Ages.' How valid is this assessment of Viking civilisation between the eighth and eleventh centuries?

Once your proposed question has been approved by WJEC senior moderators, work on your NEA can begin in earnest.

Summary

- Make sure that the topic in your question is a recognisable or mainstream issue.
- Make sure that your question reflects a clear historical debate about the issue set in the question.
- Make sure that your question contains an evaluative term that enables you to make a valid and supported judgement.
- Make sure that you can access a sufficient range of primary or contemporary material to be able to evaluate the evidence base effectively.
- Make sure that you don't choose a question that overlaps with the content of the Depth Study you are studying.

◼ How is your essay assessed?

The NEA at WJEC is essentially an exercise where the component parts of the answer are integrated in order to address the question. This includes linking the evaluation of primary source material to the formation of varying interpretations.

Assessment objectives

The NEA will be assessed by your teacher, who will allocate a separate mark for each of the three AOs for GCE History. This section of the guide explains what these are and how they apply to the assessment of your NEA.

AO1

Assessment objective 1 (AO1) requires that you:

> Demonstrate, organise and communicate knowledge and understanding to analyse and evaluate the key features related to the periods studied, making substantiated judgements and exploring concepts, as relevant, of cause, consequence, change, continuity, similarity, difference and significance.

The NEA is marked out of 60 and AO1 is worth up to 15 marks — that is, 25% of the total.

When determining bands and marks for AO1, your teacher will be looking for evidence that your essay is well structured and written. In order to determine this, they will be looking for:
- a clear introduction
- frequent reference to the question posed
- a final judgement which reflects the findings of the whole essay
- integration and linkage throughout the essay as a whole
- deployment of historical knowledge which helps to advance the debate in the answer

Your teacher does not want to see an answer which simply describes or narrates general historical content or is a series of unlinked questions.

Tip

To gain credit for AO1 you will need to provide a clearly focused introduction, show linkage in your answer, use appropriate historical knowledge and reach a final judgement.

AO2

Assessment objective 2 (AO2) requires that you:

> Analyse and evaluate appropriate source material, primary and/or contemporary to the period, within its historical context.

AO2 is also worth up to 15 marks — 25% of the total.

When determining bands and marks for AO2, your teacher will be looking to reward:
- your ability to evaluate primary or contemporary sources within their historical context
- your research skills in finding a number of primary and/or contemporary source materials — normally between 6 and 8 in number

Tip

To gain credit for AO2, you should select a range of 6–8 sources and evaluate these for their contribution in showing how and why the historical debate over the issue has developed.

- your ability to analyse the sources selected to help explain the formation and test the validity of different interpretations
- use of your source evaluation skills to show how the selected sources may have influenced the making of at least two contrasting or differing interpretations by historians

AO3

Assessment objective 3 (AO3) requires that you:

> Analyse and evaluate, in relation to the historical context, different ways in which aspects of the past have been interpreted.

AO3 is worth up to 30 marks — that is, 50% of the total.

When determining bands and marks for AO3, your teacher will be looking to reward:

- your understanding of the developing historical debate on the issue set in the question
- your understanding of the reasons why historical interpretations change over time and how a debate over the issue set has developed over time
- your understanding that interpretations are generally valid when made, but are also open to challenge and to change and development over time as different historians enter a debate over the issues
- discussion of the validity of the evidence base — which is crucially how AO2 and AO3 are linked in the NEA and why an integrated approach is the best way to tackle the assessment

Tip

To gain credit for AO3 you should show understanding of how and why the historical debate over the issue set in the question has developed.

Understanding the mark scheme

In this section we will look at how your teacher will apply the marks available in the marking scheme. These will be applied in relation to how well you can address the criteria which define the assessment objectives as laid down in the mark scheme.

An understanding of the criteria which define the assessment objectives in the mark scheme will help you to be aware of what you need to demonstrate to achieve the higher bands and marks. At the outset you need to understand that the NEA is designed to encourage you to produce an independent and individual response which answers the question set. Such a response is judged in its totality but in particular your teacher will be looking at your response to see how well the mark scheme criteria have been met.

The accredited and published mark scheme for the NEA can be found in the specification for WJEC GCE History and in Appendix 1 at the end of this book.

As with all other mark schemes for the units that make up WJEC GCE History, the mark scheme for the NEA is laid down in six hierarchical bands, each with agreed criteria which define the three different AOs that are assessed in the NEA. This is known as a level of response mark scheme. The criteria in the mark scheme define the qualities that are expected to be seen in work for each AO.

Applying the mark scheme

When assessing your essay, your teacher will first use the guidance from WJEC to place the essay into one of the six bands based on the mark scheme.

Your teacher has been provided with specific guidance in three particular areas:

■ The assessment of your essay must first be led by the assessment of the criteria related to AO3. This is because AO3 carries 50% of the available marks and also because the main requirement of the NEA is to consider, in relation to the historical context, different ways in which aspects of the past have been interpreted.

■ The marks and bands awarded for AO1 and AO2 should not exceed that given for AO3. This will prevent candidates from being given too much credit for answers that focus too much on description or mere deployment of knowledge, and thus do not focus on answering the question in an integrated way.

Your teacher has also been advised to ensure that, when applying the mark scheme, they credit essays that show how the range of primary and contemporary sources selected provides evidence that allows different interpretations to be created. You must therefore demonstrate the ability to evaluate a range of sources in their historical context and discuss the developing historical debate connected with the chosen topic. Historical context means both the situation in which the source material was produced and its relationship to the question being answered.

What do the bands mean?

In the mark scheme, the weakest responses are placed in Band 1 and the very best are placed in Band 6. In order to understand the nature of each band, it is vital to remember that interpretations are the judgements that historians make about historical events. Your selected question will contain an interpretation of an issue or development which has to be assessed for its validity alongside at least one alternative interpretation.

Band 1

Band 1 is awarded for essays that show only some use of the selected sources to discuss the interpretation presented in the question. Answers graded at Band 1 will focus only on the interpretation set in the question and fail to mention or deal with any other possible interpretations.

Band 2

Band 2 is awarded for demonstrating some knowledge and understanding of the interpretation set in the question and at least some awareness of another possible interpretation. At Band 2, your teacher will not expect to find any valid reasoning as to why these interpretations differ. They will award the lower marks of Band 2 for an essay which is a narrative on the topic and/or a descriptive account of the historiography associated with the issue set in the question.

Tip

Avoid a name-dropping approach when attempting to discuss how and why different interpretations are formed. This is very formulaic and is really deploying knowledge for knowledge's sake.

Band 3

Band 3 essays usually employ a range of primary sources to illustrate aspects of the interpretation provided in the question and at least one alternative interpretation. These essays are largely based on source evaluation and label the sources as being 'useful' or 'valuable' to the interpretations mentioned, rather than demonstrating any real understanding of how the sources can be linked to the development of the historical debate. Band 3 essays will also largely use the sources to show that the reasons why interpretations differ is that they are written by different historians. They will not show clear awareness of how and why the selection of sources by historians can demonstrate the developing historical debate.

Tip

Band 3 responses are often written using a mechanistic or formulaic approach, with answers often presented in discrete sections.

Band 4

To gain a Band 4 mark, you must demonstrate some evidence of using source evaluation skills to discuss not only the interpretation set in the question and other possible interpretations, but also some relevant issues concerning the development of the historical debate about the issue in the question. Band 4 marks will be awarded for some evaluation of the selected sources — for example, commenting on their value, utility, reliability or bias — to address the question set regarding the validity of a particular interpretation. At Band 4, your teacher will expect and accept some generalised comments about why differences in interpretations occur — such as the changing evidence base or the emergence of different schools of history at different times.

Bands 5 and 6

To gain a mark at either Band 5 or Band 6 you will have to integrate your response to meet the requirements of AO2 and AO3 especially. You should be able to show from your range of sources *how* and *why* a historian would find a source of some value as evidence for creating or supporting a particular interpretation. You should discuss the validity of a number of alternative interpretations (at least two) and discuss a range of valid reasons why the historical debate has changed over time. You should also make a focused judgement, clearly addressing the validity of the interpretation given in the question. The decision made by the teacher as to which band to place the response in will be based on the quality of the integration attempted and the quality of the judgement on validity that you offer.

Tip

Band 6 responses must analyse and evaluate the chosen primary sources to discuss the validity of a number of alternative interpretations (at least two) and discuss a range of valid reasons to show how the historical debate has developed over time.

Summary

- Your NEA is assessed using all three of the assessment objectives for GCE History.
- For AO1 your answer needs to be well structured and provide a substantiated judgement on the question set.
- For AO2 you need to show how primary sources may have influenced the making of different interpretations by historians.
- For AO3 you should show understanding of how a debate amongst historians over the issue set has developed over time.

◼ Working independently

Before beginning the NEA, it is vital that the roles of both your teacher and yourself are clarified. Your NEA has to be both *individual* and *independent*.

- ◼ *Individual* — the work produced has to be your own, not that of a group or done with another person.
- ◼ *Independent* — the work has to be produced by yourself; others can have a degree of input but this should be at a general advisory level.

Due to these definitions, the role of your teacher in the NEA is very different from that permitted in the other units of the course which are examined externally.

The role of the teacher

Your teacher has a vital role to play in helping to prepare you for your NEA task. Clear guidelines are laid down to define what your teacher's role in the process can be.

What can teachers provide for students before they begin their NEA work?

Before you begin to research and construct your response, your teacher may discuss with you and your fellow students general areas such as:

- ◼ analysing and evaluating primary sources
- ◼ testing the validity of different interpretations
- ◼ constructing and structuring an essay
- ◼ the value of planning and record keeping

Your teacher should offer you and your classmates a general skills-based session discussing and demonstrating the methods and skills of a historian, including methods of research, methods of evidence gathering and data handling, analysing and evaluating sources, and making judgements about the validity of interpretations.

This general skills-based session should also cover the work of historians in creating interpretations and approaches to the analysis and evaluation of different historical interpretations. In this session your teacher is allowed to outline the main historical debates in relation to the approved NEA questions, and this may include advising you about or discussing possible areas of information, including the availability of primary evidence and different interpretations. This should take no more than about two or three lessons and should be offered to you before you start on your NEA essay.

Your teacher should make you aware that in your essay you need to be able to identify and discuss a range of interpretations, including the work of at least two historians or schools of history. Your teacher should also ensure that you are aware of the requirement to use your selected range of primary sources to show evidence for the interpretation(s) discussed.

Teachers may also organise visits to libraries and archives and arrange lectures from visiting speakers and other group activities if appropriate.

While your work progresses, your teacher can:

- ensure that you are advised how to make use of books, articles, source and document packs, libraries, record offices and the internet, as appropriate, to develop research and evidence-gathering skills
- encourage you to keep a file to retain any rough notes and materials as evidence of work done independently and to verify the exercise
- support you in the development of enquiry and presentation skills, such as effective record keeping and referencing and planning skills
- exercise supervision over your work — but they must not make suggestions for improvements or amendments to the draft of your answer beyond pointing out the assessment criteria in the mark scheme

Your role

Once your teacher has introduced the NEA and taught the general skills-based session, you can begin planning and researching for your NEA in earnest.

Your planning and research can be scheduled in lesson time, in your own time, or as a combination of both. However, you must write your answer as an individual exercise and your teacher has to authenticate the work as being wholly your work. It would be reasonable for your teacher to be aware of your progress, but you may undertake a considerable amount of the exercise without direct supervision, provided that the teacher is confident that the work produced is your own. You will also be expected to sign a declaration stating that the work submitted is entirely your own.

What you need to do — in a nutshell

You, as an individual and independent learner, need to:

- research and find, analyse and evaluate a range of primary and/or contemporary evidence relevant to your chosen question
- research and find at least two differing or contrasting historical interpretations of the set issue in your chosen question
- explain the issue in the context of the developing historical debate
- explain how and why there are differences in historical interpretations over the set issue in your chosen question
- ensure that your answer focuses on the exact question set
- ensure that you provide a substantiated judgement on the set issue
- ensure that your answer is coherent, lucid, integrated and concise
- complete your answer in 3,000–4,000 of your own words
- ensure that the sources you use are fully attributed and placed appropriately
- use ICT in your research and in the presentation of your answer

> **Tip**
>
> Teachers are not allowed to provide much for you in material terms. They must not provide a document pack or detailed notes on the set enquiries, as learners are expected to research the issue and produce their response individually and independently.

> **Tip**
>
> Remember that the work produced has to be your own; your teacher can have a degree of input but this should only be at a general advisory level.

Summary

- Your NEA has to be both *individual* and *independent*.
- Your teacher can offer a general skills-based session where they discuss and demonstrate the methods and skills of a historian.
- Your teacher can exercise supervision over your work and offer general advice.
- You must write the essay as an individual exercise in lesson time, in your own time, or as a combination of both.

■ Defining source material

Before you begin your NEA work in earnest, it is important to define the nature of the source material that you will need to find, analyse and evaluate.

What are primary or contemporary sources?

Primary or contemporary sources are defined as:

- any source produced contemporarily by a participant at the event/development being discussed, such as official reports, diaries, notes and jottings, letters, telegrams, briefing notes, speeches, recordings, photographs or verbatim records
- any source recorded by a contemporary who was not a participant but reflects contemporary views held of the event/development, such as cartoons, newspaper reports, posters, pamphlets, audio and visual reports and surveys
- any source which is solely factually based on data/evidence gathered during the period of the event or development, such as a summary of financial expenditure in a chart or mass observation types of records, even if presented later than the date of the set enquiry
- contemporary illustrations, engravings or woodcuts that depict actual events
- contemporary artefacts and memorabilia depicting the events being discussed

These are the raw materials on which historians will base their interpretations of the events or developments they are discussing. They can be evaluated for their value in helping to create and support a particular historical interpretation.

What is secondary material?

Secondary material is created after events and developments, usually by historians and later commentators. Such material includes:

- extracts from the work of historians and from other academic or non-academic commentators
- material that may have been subject to influences after the event/development, such as biographies, memoirs and recollections
- composed or fictional accounts, such as re-enactments, films, plays, television programmes, podcasts or novels
- artistic impressions, paintings or illustrations made after the event/development being illustrated

This type of material is made later than the event or development being discussed. These are defined as *interpretations* of the past, as they have been created with an element of subjectivity and with the benefit of hindsight. The views and attitudes expressed in this material form part of the debate that has developed over the issues being discussed in your chosen question. This material, when gathered, can be used to illustrate the development of the debate, but there is no need to evaluate this material in the same way that the primary sources are evaluated. There is a clear distinction between analysing and evaluating primary sources and discussing material that was created after the events/developments being discussed.

Tip

AO2 marks will be awarded for your ability to evaluate primary sources for their use in helping formulate and support different historical interpretations.

Tip

AO3 marks will be awarded for your ability to analyse and evaluate secondary material as part of the developing historical debate over the issue in your question. There is no need to evaluate this material in the same way that your chosen primary sources are evaluated.

Content Guidance

In order to make the distinction between material produced at the time and that produced later, it is important to use and understand the following terms:

- *Sources* — material that is primary/contemporary to the period being studied.
- *Extracts* — material relevant to the enquiry that has been created by later commentators.

Tip

'Sources' are primary and/or contemporary material, such as eyewitness accounts, letters, diary entries and comments made immediately in newspaper reports, articles, posters, cartoons, etc. 'Extracts' are taken from the later interpretations of events and developments made by historians.

Task 2

Primary or later?

The material below has been gathered in order to research an enquiry on the causes of the American Civil War. Use the definitions of sources and extracts given above to decide whether each piece of evidence is a primary source or an extract illustrating a later interpretation.

Example 1

> The war, when it came in 1861, was not primarily a conflict over state rights. It was not primarily a war born of economic grievances. It was a war over slavery and the future position of black Americans.

Allan Nevins, a leading American Civil War historian, writing in his biography of President Lincoln, *The Emergence of Lincoln* (1947)

Example 2

> If this decision stands, slavery, instead of being what the people of the slave states have hitherto called it, their 'peculiar institution', will become a Federal institution. It will be the common shame of all the States, both those that are free and those that have slaves. Wherever our flag floats, it is the flag of slavery. If so, that flag should have the light of the stars and the streaks of morning red erased from it and replaced by the whip and the chain. It will divide and destroy us.

From an editorial in a northern newspaper, the *New York Evening Post*, commenting on the Supreme Court's decision in the *Dred Scott* case (18 March 1857)

Example 3

> In the momentous step which our State has taken of dissolving its connection with the government of which we so long formed a part, it is just that we should declare the reasons: Our position is thoroughly identified with the institution of slavery. There was no choice left us but submission to abolition or a dissolution of the Union. The hostility to our institution of slavery has been shown by:
>
> - refusing the admission of new slave states into the union
> - nullifying the Fugitive Slave Law in almost every free state
> - investing with the honours of martyrdom the wretch John Brown whose purpose was to apply flames to our dwellings and the weapons of destruction to our lives

The justification for secession issued by the State of Mississippi (9 January 1861)

Example 4

> The Civil War arose from different and opposing ideas as to the nature of government. The conflict was between those who held it to be strictly federal in character and those who maintained it was thoroughly national, between the rights of the state and the rights of central government.

Alexander Stephens, vice president of the Confederacy, reflecting on the American Civil War in his book, *A Constitutional View of the Late War between the States* (1868)

What does the 'developing historical debate' mean?

The phrase 'developing historical debate' and the term 'historiography' can be considered as meaning the same thing as far as the NEA is concerned. In the criteria for Band 6 it is stated that you need to discuss the developing historiography about the issue in your question. In the mark scheme for Band 5 the phrase 'development of the historical debate' is used.

This does not mean running through a list of different historians and what they have written or said about an issue. That would be simply relaying information without making any attempt to address the set question.

Discussing the development of the historical debate means that you need to be able to show how and why different interpretations are formed and why there have been changes in the interpretation of the issue set in the question. This is part of the skill of being able to put the different interpretations of the issue in 'their historical context'. In this case, this means addressing issues such as:

■ when the interpretation was made (the context)
■ what has influenced the creator(s) of the interpretation
■ what evidence base has been used to back up the interpretation

It is reasonable to consider any schools of history that have developed with regard to the issue in your question and the contribution of leading historians in these schools. When considering changes in the interpretation of the past, you should discuss more than one school of history — but two or three will be enough.

Tip

In order to discuss the development of the historical debate, you need to be able to show how and why different interpretations of the issue set in your question have been formed.

Summary

■ Primary sources are those produced at the time of the events or developments being discussed.
■ When used in your NEA, these are called *sources*.
■ Secondary material is created after the events and developments have happened, usually by historians and later commentators.
■ If used in your NEA, these are called *extracts*.
■ Discussing the development of the historical debate means showing how and why different interpretations are formed and why there have been changes in the interpretation of the issue set in the question.

■ Planning and structuring your essay

Once you have decided on your question and your introductory lessons about the NEA have been completed, you should start to plan your answer.

Timing

One area to be aware of is timing. It is likely that you will be given considerable time to plan, draft, review and finalise your essay. Do not fall into the temptation of leaving the work on the NEA until the deadline starts to loom.

The actual period of time you are given to work on your NEA depends on your school or college and its internal arrangements, but a suggested plan is given in Table 1 which you can adapt appropriately. Remember that WJEC will have approved your question at least six weeks before you are due to begin the NEA. (Approval will usually have been received during your Year 12 studies if you are following the course over two years.)

Table 1 Time planning

What needs to be done?	When?	How long?
Basic research on the developing historical debate and available primary sources	End of Year 12; summer holidays; start of Year 13	3–4 weeks
Construction of the plan for your essay	Start of Year 13	1 week
Introduction — an answer in a nutshell	Start of Year 13	1–2 weeks
First draft of some material	Half-term in Year 13	3–4 weeks
First draft of your completed essay	First week in December	3–4 weeks
Formal review with your teacher	By Christmas break	1 week
Your review of your material	By end of January	3–4 weeks
Completion of your final essay for submission	By end of February	3–4 weeks

Task 3

Time planning

Construct a chart similar to the one above which relates to the time period that you have been given by your teacher.

In class or out of class?

The plan above gives you between 5–6 months to begin, research, draft, review and complete your work.

Given that you will also be studying for the examined units throughout Year 13 in particular, the amount of time in class that you can devote to the construction of your essay is likely to be limited. Therefore much of the work on your NEA is likely to be done outside timetabled lessons, either at home or in non-contact time. This is where you will need to use your transferable skills of independence and organisation. Your teacher will want to monitor your progress on the NEA work and advise you

Tip

Don't leave your NEA work until the deadline gets closer. Work steadily on it throughout the time available.

Tip

Build into your planning schedule time when you need to work on your NEA at home and in school or college.

appropriately during review sessions, but basically much of the time spent on the NEA will be your own.

Identifying the key historical concept in the question

You should be aware, from the discussions with your teacher in the introductory sessions, of the fundamental aspects which underpin your NEA essay. These are:

- constructing a response which addresses the issue in the question set
- discussing the validity of the interpretation given in the question within the developing historical debate surrounding the issue
- demonstrating how primary source material can be used to support the forming of different or contrasting interpretations

The first thing you need to do is to ask yourself — do I really understand what the question is asking me to do? What is the question really about? By identifying the key historical concept in your question, you will make it easier to carry out your research. Table 2 gives some examples of NEA questions that can be broken down into more simple historical concepts.

Table 2 Historical concepts

Question	Concept
'The success of the Norman invasion in 1066 was mainly due to their military superiority.' How valid is this assessment of the Norman invasion of 1066?	The causes of a historical event or development
'The Acts of Union were an instantaneous success in that they reduced Wales in the course of a single generation to a state of order and obedience to the law of England.' How valid is this assessment of the impact of the Acts of Union to 1603?	The effects of political change
Do you agree with the view that Peel was the most effective political leader in the period 1834 to 1880?	A comparison of the success of various political leaders
Do you agree that the people of Britain were mostly content and prosperous due to the post-war consensus in the years 1945 to 1964?	The extent of change over time
How far do you agree with the view that Thomas Clarkson was the most significant individual in the campaign to abolish the slave trade?	An assessment of the significance of various individuals

Task 4

Historical concepts

Can you identify the key historical concept in the following questions?

Question	Concept
Do you agree that the outcome of the Cuban Missile Crisis was more a triumph for the diplomacy of Khrushchev than that of Kennedy?	
'The lives of the Russian peasants were transformed for the better in the years between 1928 and 1964.' How valid is this assessment of the peasantry in Russia?	
How far do you agree that economic grievances were mainly responsible for causing protest and rebellion in the period 1485 to 1603?	
'Gaining the vote by 1928 was the most important turning point in the campaign for gender equality in Wales and England.' How far do you agree with this view of the changing role and status of women in the period 1890 to 1990?	
Historians disagree about the impact of the Reformation. How far do you agree that the Reformation mainly affected urban areas?	

Using a plan

Now you need to go one step further. One useful way of planning is to construct a diagram or a chart which outlines the key interpretations to discuss. You can use such a chart to give you the structure and outline that you need before you start to write your essay. This approach has three particular strengths:

- It outlines some different interpretations of the issue that you will discuss in your answer.
- It attempts to place these different interpretations within the debate over the issue.
- It suggests possible primary sources which may be researched, analysed and evaluated as evidence to support different interpretations of the issue.

In your introductory lessons to the NEA, it is worth discussing this approach with your teacher, who can confirm the suitability of your initial ideas or suggest other areas that you may wish to research. Such an approach will give clarity and structure to your research and also to the formation of your answer.

A worked example of an initial plan for a question on the unification of Italy is suggested in Table 3.

Table 3 Clarifying interpretations

Title: 'The main reason for the unification of Italy by 1861 was the willingness of the key figures to work together for a common goal.' How valid is this interpretation of the reasons for the unification of Italy by 1861?		
Different interpretations	**Where does this come in the developing debate?**	**Supporting evidence to look for**
Interpretation 1: The key figures (including Cavour, Garibaldi and Victor Emmanuel) worked together harmoniously to create the new Kingdom of Italy by 1861	The initial explanation for the founding of Italy; laid down by politicians and supported by traditional Italian historians keen to build a new nation	Portraits from the time showing the key figures together Public statements by key figures Statements by the National Society
Interpretation 2: It was the conflict between the key figures — not their willingness to cooperate — that spurred Italy on to unity by 1861	Proposed by left-wing historians in the decade after the First World War; followed by revisionist historians such as Mack-Smith and Seaman after the Second World War	Private correspondence of the key figures Recorded conversations involving the key figures Views from Britain or France or Mazzini
Interpretation 3: Social and economic changes were the main reason why demands for unification had succeeded by 1861	Post-revisionist historians since the 1960s have seen the growth of nationalism in countries such as Italy in the mid-nineteenth century as part of a movement which was continental rather than individual to a particular country	Statistics about industrial growth D'Azeglio statements Views of leading industrialists at the time

Task 5

Clarifying interpretations

Complete a chart similar to Table 3 which relates to the question that you have chosen. Use the blank grid below to help you. It may not be possible to complete it from the start, but it will provide a useful aid as you make progress.

Title:		
Different interpretations	Where does this come in the developing debate?	Supporting evidence to look for
Interpretation 1:		
Interpretation 2:		
Interpretation 3:		

Summary

- Work regularly on your NEA — don't leave it too late!
- Organising your time is essential and remember that you will have considerable opportunity to work independently.
- From the start, be clear about the key historical concept in your question — you will have to address this throughout your answer.
- Use a plan. It can be flexible but using a plan is an invaluable organising strategy.

◼ Carrying out research for your essay

For the NEA, you will need to gather information from published material when researching and completing your task. In this case, you will have unrestricted access to sources and material containing sources.

At this early stage it is worth making sure that there are sufficient accessible sources available to use. You may have chosen a fascinating issue in your question, but there may just not be the material available to show your skills, in AO2 and AO3 particularly. It is better to discover this at the start than after a few months of work when you are struggling to find material to analyse and evaluate.

Ways of gathering material

There are various ways of gathering information when researching for your essay. Some examples are given below:

- Books, articles and magazines will have been written on the issue in your chosen question. These will generally be secondary in nature, as they will be later creations and many will have focused sections outlining the historiography or the debate that has developed about the issue you have chosen to study.

Tip

Identify up to three different interpretations of the issue you are studying and try to place them within the developing historical debate. This will give a clear structure to your work.

- Your school or college or local library will be likely to have examples of this type of material ready for you to research. Centres have been encouraged to establish dedicated libraries of such material.
- While many textbooks are available in traditional paper format, increasingly you will use the internet to research material of this nature. Using a combination of both traditional and web-based research is recommended.
- You can try entering key words associated with your enquiry into a search engine. This will throw up many potential lines of enquiry — and will begin to test your ability to differentiate and evaluate the material.
- Many of the secondary books, articles and magazines written on the issue in your chosen question will be based on the use of primary sources. Many will include examples of this primary material to support and corroborate the interpretations made by the author.
- Collections of primary and contemporary material relevant to the enquiry are very valuable. These again can be in text form or web based. Sometimes you may have to pay a subscription to access such material online; sometimes it is free.
- Local authorities also have helpful archive services and record offices where material, particularly of a local nature, can be accessed.

Using the internet for research

The nature of the internet makes it the most obvious place for you to undertake research. However, the sheer size and diversity of the internet should cause you to be careful when trying to find research material. Most of the internet is not controlled or moderated, and information that you locate may be factually incorrect or unreliable. When you are using the internet to gather information about various interpretations in particular, use these points to verify the website or resource:

- Is the online resource written by an identifiable author? If an author cannot be identified, you will not be able to fully reference the source and assess its credibility.
- Has this online resource been created on behalf of an organisation or enterprise? If it has, it might have commercial, political or religious bias.
- Are contact details given for the online resource that can be checked, such as names, telephone numbers or an 'About us' link?
- Is the information in the online resource dated? Are you able to follow links? Dead links suggest that a page has not been updated recently.

Volume of material

One of the initial problems that you may experience is finding too much information about the issue you are studying, much of which will be peripheral and not directly focused. Be ruthless in your research. It is vital that, when reading the material you have accessed, you have a clear idea of whether it will fit into your plan and then you will be able to accept or reject it quickly.

Gathering a range of primary sources

In order to access marks at both AO2 and AO3, you must research and evaluate a range of primary sources which you have identified independently. You should select 6–8 primary sources to analyse and evaluate in your assessment.

Make sure that you choose a range of primary sources to evaluate. Here are some tips that you may wish to remember:

- Be clear about the definition of a 'primary' source (see p. 15).
- Your primary sources are to be analysed and evaluated in terms of how they have enabled historians to create a debate about the issue you are studying.
- It is tempting to use well-known primary sources which many other learners will also use.
- Try to find those which are slightly more obscure. This will give your work more individuality and develop your research skills as well.
- Make sure that you select a range of suitable primary sources.

A good way of checking that you are using a range of primary sources is to use a checklist such as the one below:

- official reports
- diaries/notes
- letters
- speeches
- cartoons
- newspaper reports
- posters
- pamphlets
- photographs

One key issue that you should be aware of is that any written primary source material that you select to analyse and evaluate can vary in length — there is no strict rule regarding the length that is appropriate for source material. However, it must be substantial enough to be able to provide adequate evidence for a historian making an interpretation.

Task 6

Using a range of sources

In your research, have you identified a range of sources? If you can answer 'yes' to at least four of the types of source in the list given above, it is likely that you will be able to analyse and evaluate a 'range' of different types of primary source.

Summary

- Use a variety of media to gather information and material.
- Be careful not to rely too much on the internet without verifying the origin of material.
- Become decisive in accepting or rejecting material — or you may be swamped with stuff.
- Remember that using a range of primary sources is essential.

Tip

Select a range of primary sources to analyse and evaluate, and to illustrate how the historical debate has developed.

■ Setting out an introduction

Once you have identified sources and made initial draft notes regarding the developing historical debate about the issue in your question, you can begin to construct an introduction to your essay.

Here is some basic advice to remember for your introduction:

- Show that you understand the demands of the question. This can be done by making reference to the issue in the question. Someone reading your introduction should be able to tell what the question is after a few paragraphs.
- Your introduction could define some key terms or concepts in the question or briefly set the historical context surrounding the issue.
- Outline briefly the different interpretations that make up part of the developing historical debate.
- Refer generally to some of the primary evidence base that might support the forming of different interpretations.
- Suggest your own view about the question that you are answering. This can be called 'an answer in a nutshell'. Generally this will align with the judgement in your conclusion.
- Keep your introduction short and interesting — as a rule of thumb, one side of A4 paper is ample.
- Avoid giving a narrative or description of events or developments. Narrative and descriptive writing does not gain many marks in the mark scheme.

Using the points above can help to keep you focused on addressing the chosen question in your introduction.

Tip

Despite your interest in the actual history connected with the issue in the question, don't be tempted to describe or narrate events in any detail.

Task 7

Writing introductions

Use this checklist to decide on the appropriateness of the introductions that follow:

- Can you tell what the question is from reading the introduction?
- Does the introduction refer to different interpretations?
- Does the introduction mention the evidence base?
- Does the introduction suggest an answer to the question set?

Introduction 1

The origins of the First World War, the most colossal war the world had yet seen, undoubtedly stemmed from chains of confusion, misunderstanding and unintended consequences of developments and events between the Triple Entente and the Triple Alliance, which historians continue to debate more than a century later, with little consensus. The First World War, which was to kill 10 million people, has never vanished from Europe's memory.

The BBC comedy *Blackadder Goes Forth* provides a comedic outlook of Great Power imperialism in its 1989 episode 'Goodbyeee', which induced war. The power of satire in augmenting the duplicity of Great Britain and France is invaluable, albeit written jocularly. Britain and France stupefied in impotence amidst the inherently threatening and dangerous expansion of Kaiser Wilhelm II's Germany, notwithstanding the reality that the Kaiser's actual empire of land grabbing in the nineteenth century had, in actual fact, been very limited in Africa. It was more the fact that the Kaiser was expanding Germany's military forces, especially her sea power, which had been the domain of Britain, that was the real concern. Clever in its delivery though it may be, the episode is simplistic, with a lack of clarity, and indeed it is arguably only amusing to those with an historical understanding of the period, otherwise the jokes and anecdotes would actually make little sense.

The Kaiser's imperialist appetite, which is evident in this episode, can be seen most powerfully and most dramatically in his disregard for the terms of the Treaty of London. Signed by Britain and the Kaiser's grandfather Kaiser Wilhelm I in 1839, amongst others, the effort of European peace is explicit in the official document, in guaranteeing the neutrality of the newly created state of Belgium. Seemingly, the treaty highlights that European powers then did not strive for war, until the accession of Kaiser Wilhelm I's grandson in 1888, upon the early death of Friedrich III, whose role in plunging the world into a cataclysmic war was devastating. Indeed it was the invasion of Belgium by the Kaiser in August 1914 that precipitated the entry of Britain and then her allies in the Triple Entente, to declare war. What the Kaiser had done had not only violated the independence of a sovereign nation but in so doing, had also violated international law, of which his own country had been a signatory. This wilful disregard of the sanctity of international law surely shows that the Kaiser deserves his reputation as a cruel warmonger and the subsequently high death toll and the devastation and destruction of much of Belgium in the Flanders area is a clear testament to this fact. Certainly the invasion inspired many British men to join up in 1914.

Introduction 2

The regime in Fascist Italy between 1922 and 1945 was one of the most significant threads of early twentieth-century dictatorship, born out of the First World War and characterising the Second. Mussolini's Italy was the earliest example of a right-wing dictatorship, being an influence on Hitler's regime in Germany, and the Allies opposed it as they opposed everything it stood for. Mussolini had a personality cult following and was the undisputed leader of a one-party police state, but when it is examined the question is raised as to whether his regime was truly totalitarian in the strictest sense of the word. Postwar commentary on this subject stressed the powerful and repressive nature of his regime — history was at this time being written by the victorious Allies, advocates of democracy who were not about to be sympathetic to the government of their defeated adversaries. A marked difference needed to be shown between their nations to justify the cost of war. Max Gallo writes in 1964 that the regime was 'thoroughly Fascist', so that 'special supervision was the fate...of all Italians'. However, historians such as Philip Morgan in 1995 and Martin Clark in 1996, comparing Fascist Italy to Nazi Germany or to Stalin's Russia, have found that Mussolini's regime was the least totalitarian of the three.

To consider this question, it is first necessary to consider what is meant by the word 'totalitarian', to make it possible to compare different aspects of the regime to this definition and come to a viable conclusion. In his book *The European Dictatorships 1918–1945*, Stephen J. Lee sets out four qualifications of a truly totalitarian state. Firstly, there must be an ideology which all parts of life are subservient to and 'society [should be] restructured according to its goals'. This ideology should be akin to a religion or even a cult in the way that it is treated by its participants. Secondly, there must be a single party in control of the political system and no possibility of another to supersede it, 'presided over by a leader who was invested with the cult of personality'. Thirdly, 'the individual was completely subordinated to the dictates of the state through a process of coercion and indoctrination'. This includes both terror and indoctrination through 'the shaping of education, literature, art and music to the objectives of political ideology'. Finally, the state must have complete control over the economy.

Introduction 3

The First World War was a poignant moment in history. The leaders involved in this war — particularly on its Western Front — were operating in the period of mass armies with unforeseen developments. This brought with it considerable challenges that would shape the nature of warfare in the twentieth century. This may therefore account for the changing historical interpretation of the leadership in the First World War throughout the twentieth century. The mass element of the war dictated how the army would be directed and draws heavy focus to administrative decision making at the top in the interpreting of events.

There has been much debate surrounding the regard for human life shown by the generals on the Western Front, especially when compared with the brave, honest conduct of ordinary soldiers. The metaphor of 'lions led by donkeys' has been used to distinguish between leaders and soldiers and is certainly an accurate one to those historians and later commentators who detested the incompetency of the generals whose actions discarded the lives of undaunted boys and their pals who fought for their country.

Yet surely the nature of this war was unforeseen. The leaders on both sides could not comprehend the innovative force that would befall the battlefield and the experiences that would plague literature and film thereafter, told through a traumatised populace who came to lose so much. During the First World War, the military leadership was actually acclaimed for its skill and organisation. In the long years of the war, newspapers heralded the greatness of military leaders, responding to the public appetite for glory. This established a popular tradition of heroic infallibility and an ignorance of contemporary military theory. Even a decade after the war, opinion remained relatively positive. Thousands flocked to the funeral of General Haig, to commemorate his life and recognise him as another 'victim' of the war. However, with the rise of postwar poetry publications like the work of Wilfred Owen, providing a raw and unadulterated account of the reality of war, critical opinion and military disenchantment surfaced. Much like later debunking of myths originating during the war by historians, these accounts contradicted the myth of glory ('the old lie, dulce et decorum est pro patria mori') that had taken in a credulous public. David Lloyd George's memoirs exposed the misplaced trust in Haig. Amid a climate of pacifism alongside historians like Alan Clark who coined the phrase first said by Hindenburg, 'lions led by donkeys', A.J.P. Taylor was highly critical of First World War leadership. It was only later that an era of revisionist historical interpretation was brought in by Keegan and Terraine. Recent interpretations have sought to re-evaluate the actions of the Generals and consider how they were responsible for implementation of great innovation.

Each of these schools of thought has evolved as historians have selected and explored evidence from the time — evidence which is open to interpretation and which can be utilised to support varying interpretations of whether 'lions led by donkeys' is a valid assessment of the British army on the Western Front during the First World War.

Historical interpretations and the developing historical debate

Once you have constructed a draft introduction containing the elements suggested, you can begin the process of supporting your answer. It is suggested that you now build a structure based around two to three different interpretations of the issue in your question. The plan suggested on p. 20 should already have given you a number of potential interpretations. The key to success in this area centres on two aspects discussed earlier:

- The system of approving your question will have ensured that there are a variety of different interpretations on the issue you are writing about.
- Credit is given to essays which are clearly focused on discussing the developing historical debate surrounding the interpretations and sources you have selected to answer your question.

An essential element of a successful answer to the NEA is that you demonstrate understanding and awareness of the range of historical interpretations and debates that have developed in connection with the question that you have chosen to answer. This element reflects AO3, which expects you to analyse and evaluate, in relation to the historical context, different ways in which aspects of the past have been interpreted. The WJEC descriptors for Band 6 give a clear indication of what is expected of you in order to address the expectations of AO3.

- You are able to discuss the question set in the context of alternative interpretations.
- You are able to consider the validity of the interpretations in terms of the development of the historiographical context.

- You are able to demonstrate an understanding of how and why this issue has been interpreted in different ways.
- You are able to discuss how and why a particular historian or school of history would form an interpretation based on the evidence in the sources used.

To address this element of the NEA fully, it is important that you show an understanding of the formation and development of different historical interpretations and how they fit into the developing debate on the issue.

How are historical interpretations formed?

Many people believe that the study of history is largely about learning lists of dates, names and facts. It is true that the study of history contains 'stuff' which is factual and beyond doubt — the Tonypandy Riots were in 1910; the NHS was set up in 1948; the first man landed on the moon in 1969. However, the study of history involves more than this. The job of historians is to make sense of the facts, to think critically about the reasons for and the results of the facts and to form their own interpretations based on the available evidence.

One other point to remember is that historians will usually have access to a similar range of information and evidence, but some will end up reaching different interpretations or conclusions about historical developments or events. This makes all history provisional — there are nearly always different answers to the same question. These are called interpretations. The key to your NEA is that you recognise at least two of these different answers or interpretations and that you can judge them for their validity.

Your NEA gives you an opportunity to analyse and evaluate a range of different interpretations and to assess these to see if they are valid and fair ways of looking at the issue in the question you are answering.

For example, there is only one answer to the question: *When did the First World War begin?* — the answer is 1914. But is there only one answer to the question: *'The main reason for the outbreak of war in 1914 was aggressive German action.' How valid is this assessment of the outbreak of war in 1914?* Definitely not. Different historians would argue about this question and reach different interpretations about the relative importance of the reasons for the outbreak of war. These interpretations could have an element of agreement or they could vary markedly — all part of the nature of studying history.

Reasons why historians may have different interpretations

One issue which you will have addressed in other aspects of your GCE History course — probably in Unit 2 — is to discuss generally why it is possible for historians to form different interpretations of the same developments and events. There are several possible reasons, as discussed below.

Time or context

History is a popular area of study and each generation tends to look back at historical events in different ways. Values and expectations change and the events that make up history are seen in different ways. The sense of perspective also changes as events become more distant. Additionally, at times of significant anniversaries or new

Tip

Make sure that you demonstrate understanding and awareness of the range of historical interpretations and debates that have developed in connection with the question that you have chosen to answer.

happenings, historical developments often get reassessed. If you are studying the views of a particular historian or school of thought, it is important to know when they were active and the context they operated in.

Example: Cecil Rhodes

British historians writing during the time of the later British Empire tended to see Rhodes as a positive figure who played a leading role in the British dominance of southern Africa by the late nineteenth century. They focused particularly on his economic and educational legacy in southern Africa. Attitudes to imperial figures such as Rhodes began to change from the 1950s as the winds of nationalism blew stronger on the African continent. Historians began to reassess the legacy of figures such as Rhodes, who was increasingly seen as a negative and destructive force with clear racist and supremacist attitudes. This culminated in a highly publicised debate about the appropriateness of a statue of Rhodes at Oriel College in Oxford. There is, of course, a compromise school of thought which argues that Rhodes was a product of his time, convinced that the extension of British rule was commensurate with human progress, and that he used this to justify his methods, both in business and in politics.

Background and attitudes

Historians are not all the same. They have different experiences, political leanings, nationalities, upbringings and education, each of which may influence the way in which they interpret history. Your NEA is *not* an opportunity to narrate the life histories of different historians, but background factors are sometimes of value in analysing the validity of certain interpretations.

Example: the French Revolution

In general terms, left-wing or Marxist historians tend to emphasise the problems and issues that affect the lower classes. These include ownership of wealth and capital, economic inequalities and the conditions and grievances of workers. Many left-wing historians suggest that the French Revolution was caused by working-class dissatisfaction, the unfairness of feudalism in France, gross social and economic inequality and political exclusion. Historians with right-wing or conservative views may instead focus on economic freedom and opportunity and the failures of radicalism. These historians suggest the French Revolution was triggered by exaggerated grievances and falsehoods; the revolution tried to achieve too much too quickly and descended into a series of violent power struggles.

Audience

Historians write for different audiences and for different purposes. When evaluating the validity of different interpretations, the audience or purpose needs to be considered. This is often a factor that needs to be taken into account if an interpretation is expressed, for example, as a representation in a television programme or a film.

Example: Blackadder Goes Forth

Television programmes such as *Blackadder Goes Forth* have had a major impact on the way the First World War has been recently perceived in the UK. Some commentators have criticised the portrayal of the war in programmes like this for trivialising events and being full of misrepresentations — of the bungling generals, for instance. Other commentators have been much more accepting of these programmes, seeing them as primarily entertainment but also as valuable ways of capturing the imagination of learners and of encouraging them to engage with the past. The real issue is that programmes such as *Blackadder Goes Forth* are interpretations of the war, written by people who were not there, and they should be seen as part of the developing historical debate about the First World War.

Specialisation

Historians often have a particular interest in the issue being studied and will focus on a particular aspect when making their interpretations. Some may focus on economic aspects, some on political, some on social or cultural. This will often have a bearing on their final interpretation.

Example: Tudor protests and rebellions

It is possible for historians to emphasise different factors as being primarily responsible for events and developments. An example is the factors that led to protest and rebellions in the Tudor period. One school of thought is that the primary cause of such protest was economic pressure. Historians taking this view can cite protests such as the Cornish rebellion against Henry VII, the Pilgrimage of Grace in 1536 and Kett's rebellion in 1549 as examples to support their interpretations. Another group of historians may claim that the main cause of protest was political, emphasising dissatisfaction with ministers and advisers, Mary's marriage arrangements and the political ambitions of the Northern Earls. There is also a school of thought that argues that religion was the most overt factor in the rebellions. Revolts against Henry VIII criticised his choice of bishops and his treatment of the monasteries, and there was strong religious influence in the Wyatt rebellion in 1554 and that of the Northern Earls in 1559.

Availability of evidence

If an interpretation is to be considered valid, it has to be firmly based on evidence. The availability of historical evidence, especially from the time being studied, allows historians to gain an insight into the period and to formulate and propose their interpretations. Sometimes, new forms of primary evidence come to light which can alter the interpretations of historians. One other factor to bear in mind is that historians also have the ability to be selective with the evidence that they use to support their interpretations.

Example: the Cold War

All historical interpretations should be based on evidence which is as varied and widespread as possible to allow a balanced view to emerge. However, much historical data is lost, either by accident or deliberately, or perhaps because of decisions based on space or level of interest. On the other hand, sometimes historians are not able to access evidence that later becomes available to other historians. At certain times, documents are discovered or publicised that give new views of well-established events. Material may be kept secret by governments for a given period, often to protect information vital for national security. When these archives are made available, they can alter the historical perspective on an event. For example, following the collapse of the Soviet Union in 1991, a huge range of Soviet archives were made accessible, and historians were able to examine a lot more evidence on the causes of the Cold War.

Hindsight

The process of looking back at history with the knowledge of what has happened since the actual events is called hindsight — it can be a useful tool as a historian writing later can look back with more knowledge than one writing nearer the time. In this way, the degree of hindsight can be a major factor in accounting for different interpretations.

As you begin to consider the issues raised by the question that you have chosen, you need to bear in mind the general points expressed above. Most of these will be relevant to your enquiry and should form part of the evaluation of the different interpretations that you will test in your work.

Tip

Make sure that you understand why it is possible for historians to form different interpretations about the same developments and events.

Task 8

Reasons for differing interpretations

How many of the reasons why historians may have different interpretations apply to the issue in your NEA question?

Summary

- The explanation of history is provisional — it is an on-going dialogue which historians will continue to debate regularly.
- Historians will have different perspectives on the past — many of these will involve similar interpretations but others will contradict them.
- The interpretations of historians vary for many reasons — some of these will be relevant to your attempt to judge the validity of different interpretations of your issue.

Examples of differing interpretations

Here are some examples of NEA questions and varying ways in which the issues they raise have been interpreted by historians and later authors. These can match up with the planning grid suggested on p. 20.

Example 1

'The threat of revolution was the main factor behind the passing of the Reform Act of 1832.' How valid is this assessment of the passing of the Reform Act of 1832?

Historians have formed different historical interpretations of the Reform Act crisis and there has been a developing debate over this issue. Different interpretations may include:

- The Reform Act was passed mainly to prevent revolution by the working class.
- The Reform Act was passed mainly to rectify the abuses of the electoral system.
- The Reform Act was passed mainly in order to recognise the power of the growing middle class.

Example 2

'The main reason for industrial unrest in Wales between 1900 and 1914 was the growing power of the trade unions.' Do you agree with this assessment of the causes of industrial unrest in Wales between 1900 and 1914?

Historians have formed different historical interpretations of industrial unrest in Wales between 1900 and 1914 and there has been a developing debate over this issue. Different interpretations may include:

- Industrial unrest at this time was created mainly by the growth and impact of trade unions.
- Industrial unrest at this time was caused mainly by worsening working conditions after 1900.
- Industrial unrest at this time was caused mainly by the attitude and policies of the owners of mines and factories.

Example 3

Do you agree that it was the influence of the Enlightenment that was largely responsible for the outbreak of the French Revolution in 1789?

Historians have formed different historical interpretations of the reasons for the outbreak of the French Revolution in 1789 and there has been a developing debate over this issue. Varying interpretations may include:

- The French Revolution was largely caused by the influence of the Enlightenment.
- The French Revolution was largely caused by the weaknesses of the *ancien régime*.
- The French Revolution was largely caused by the financial problems of the 1770s and 1780s.

Example 4

Do you agree that the election of Lincoln as president was the main cause of the American Civil War?

Historians have formed different historical interpretations of the causes of the American Civil War and there has been a developing debate over this issue. Varying interpretations may include:

- The Civil War broke out mainly due to the election of Lincoln in 1860.
- The Civil War broke out mainly because of the long-term issue of slavery.
- The Civil War broke out mainly due to disagreements over states' rights.

Using interpretations by historians in your essay

It has to be stressed again that the NEA is not an opportunity to write all you know about the topic in the question. Neither is it an exercise to be tackled in discrete sections — something that you have been advised against in an earlier part of this guide.

Reflect again on Assessment Objective 3:

> Analyse and evaluate, in relation to the historical context, different ways in which aspects of the past have been interpreted.

Tip

Identifying at least two clear interpretations of the issue in your question should be one of your first tasks. It really isn't that difficult — one interpretation is even given in the question for you! It is then your job to find out more information about these interpretations — who has said them, why they have made them and what is their evidence base.

Remember also that half the marks available for the NEA are for demonstrating your ability with regard to AO3.

Your NEA is most of all an exercise about gauging how the value of the source material that you have selected for your essay would have contributed to the developing debate amongst historians over the issue you are tackling. It is not primarily about *what* different historians or schools of history had to say, but about *why* they said it, in view of the range of factors that could explain the making of interpretations. These factors include the availability of evidence, the political, social and economic influences on a school of history, and the influence of other historians as well as how and why the historical debate has developed.

The issue is not one of identifying interpretations as right or wrong or summarising the different views of historians. Instead you need to demonstrate an understanding that interpretations are provisional and have changed over time for a variety of reasons.

It is good practice early on to create a draft outline of the developing historical debate over the issue and how this has developed. This will form the framework of your later work, analysing and evaluating the primary material that you have found which can be used to support different schools of thought.

Testing the validity of different historical interpretations

Once you have gathered information about different interpretations and gained an understanding of the developing historical debate about the issue posed in your question, you can proceed to evaluate the validity or accuracy of some of the interpretations that form part of that debate. The opportunity to evaluate the validity or accuracy of different interpretations will be clearly offered by your chosen question. Here are two examples of the types of question approved for the NEA which offer you the opportunity to judge their validity:

- 'The New Deal was highly effective in improving the lives of the American people in the 1930s.' *How valid is this interpretation of* the New Deal?
- *Do you agree with the interpretation that* Peel was the most effective political leader in the period 1834 to 1880?

The key command phrases in these types of question are in italics above:

- How valid is this interpretation of…
- Do you agree with the interpretation that…

Both these command phrases invite you to enter into a debate about the validity or accuracy of an interpretation connected with the issue that you have chosen to study.

Presumably the historian or the school of thought that you are analysing has made a clear interpretation about the issue in the question — for example: *'The New Deal was highly effective in improving the lives of the American people in the 1930s.' How valid is this interpretation of the New Deal?*

If you were answering this question, you would have carried out research to identify a historian or a group of historians that has made such an interpretation of the New Deal policies of the 1930s. You would now need to assess the validity or accuracy of this particular interpretation.

In order to do this, you might wish to consider some of the following questions:

- Can you clearly summarise or state the interpretation made by the historian(s) about the New Deal?
- Does this interpretation belong to a particular school of thought about the New Deal? (*Tip*: be careful about using labels such as 'traditionalist' or 'revisionist' if you are not sure whether they apply.)
- Have the historian(s) approached their interpretation of the New Deal from a particular perspective, such as political, social or economic? (*Tip*: the title of the book or article is worth considering here.)
- What types of primary source are available to the historian(s) who are making this interpretation of the New Deal? (*Tip*: make sure you identify a range of appropriate primary sources that would have enabled the historian(s) to support their interpretation.)
- How would the historian(s) be able to use such primary sources to help form their interpretation of the New Deal? (*Tip*: look at pp. 46–48 for advice on how to integrate the analysis and evaluation of primary sources into your answer.)
- Are these historian(s) writing for a particular audience? (*Tip*: consider aspects such as the title of the book or article, the style of writing or the medium in which the interpretation was published.)
- Are these historian(s) writing for a particular purpose? (*Tip*: is there a particular angle or vested interest that he or she is trying to enhance — for example, nationalist bias, deliberate provocation, entertainment or commissioned work?)

Once you have considered some of these aspects, you can address the issue of the validity of the particular interpretation presented in your question. You can also use the same approach for different interpretations of the same issue.

Using extracts from the works of historians

Here it is important to refer back to the advice given on pp. 15–16. This defined any quotations or excerpts from the work of the historians studied as *extracts* — material relevant to the enquiry that has been created by later commentators.

Many students are tempted to use extracts from the historians they are studying in their answers. This is usually done to illustrate the arguments that the historian is making. In fact, there is no requirement for you to include extracts in your essay as the full range of marks at AO3 can be awarded without the inclusion of extracts. There is, however, some justification for using extracts provided they go beyond just summarising the historian's view. It is reasonable to use extracts from historians where they contribute to the discussion — for example, to use a key passage from one historian to show how that historian belongs to a school of history or to show how schools of thought have evolved.

If you do need to use extracts to show how the school of thought has developed, you should limit yourself to between two and four extracts in your answer. By following this advice you will be better able to focus on the value of the primary and contemporary evidence in helping to create different interpretations, rather than summarising what historians had to say about the issue.

A final word of warning

Many students tend to treat extracts from historians in the same way as they treat primary or contemporary material: for example, by commenting on their usefulness or reliability. *You should avoid this.* Evaluation of extracts for their utility or reliability often leads to spurious and misinformed comments on the veracity or accuracy of the historian making the interpretation.

There are no marks for source evaluation comments on the extracts from historians and therefore there is no validity in considering the bias, reliability, veracity or otherwise of such extracts.

Task 9

The forming of different interpretations

Read these examples of draft work which attempt to focus on the forming of different interpretations. Consider whether they are effective in focusing on the forming of different interpretations.

You could use the checklist in the summary on p. 36 to help you evaluate the responses.

Example 1

An example of an historian who belongs to a particular school of thought on this issue is Gary Sheffield, appointed the first professor of War Studies at the University of Birmingham in 2006. In an article written for the BBC in 2011, Sheffield argues that General Haig led a 'formidable fighting force' and the ability and experience of Haig and his fellow generals was a key reason for the success of British forces. Sheffield is representative of a group of historians who have sought to restore the reputation of the British generals as competent leaders. Such historians tend to take a more balanced view of the role played by the generals than that of the traditional school of thought or the 'lions led by donkeys' interpreters.

Sheffield's interpretation is a legacy of the influential work in the early 1960s of John Terraine, especially his work *Haig: the Educated Soldier.* Sheffield began his academic career as an undergraduate at Leeds University where he was also heavily influenced by the work of Peter Simkins, who was then working as Head of Research at the Imperial War Museum. Simkins was also among the school of historians that argued that the generals played a major role in British success and that the interpretation of 'lions led by donkeys' is now too simplistic and can be challenged both factually and objectively.

Historians of the school of thought that encompasses Terraine, Simkins and Sheffield would have had access to a range of primary and contemporary sources which they could have used to advance their arguments.

Example 2

This extract from Ian Kershaw highlights Hitler's ability to captivate and inspire the German people by the way he spoke. This puts emphasis on the importance of Hitler as a persuasive force, lessening the value of attractive policy to creating the popularity of the Nazi party. The extract suggests that as long as Hitler's audience shared his basic political feelings, he could inspire them. This suggests that policies such as economic policy worked as a stepping stone but it was Hitler himself who went on to create popularity from the basic beliefs that he and the public shared. The content within this extract enhances the validity of Intentionalist ideas regarding the popularity of the Nazi party due to the insight it gives into Hitler's persuasive style and his ability to inspire.

Kershaw would have had access to a wide range of evidence, both Intentionalist and Structuralist, when forming his opinion rather than historians writing in an earlier period, justifying his conclusion of a combination of factors being responsible for the popularity of the Nazi regime.

Example 3

Historians such as John Terraine can be described as revisionist. Terraine worked for the BBC for many years, becoming associate producer and screen writer on the TV series, *The Great War*. He is a prolific author of military history books, many concerned with the First World War. He was the founder president of the Western Front Association, dedicated to the memory of those who fought in the war. He is most noted for his defence of Haig throughout many of his books. Having a passion for the military (he made two unsuccessful attempts to join up), he is probably keen to portray the British army in a positive light. His defence of Haig could be an attempt at stirring up controversy rather than a genuine evaluation of Haig based on evidence.

His book has a close focus on the events of the Somme and because of this he would have spent more time researching this than Laffin who wrote in a more general book. His book was written much earlier than Laffin's, indicating that Terraine may not have had access to the same wealth of information.

Summary

In order to make a substantiated judgement about the validity or accuracy of an interpretation, you could try using the following checklist:
- Have you identified the particular interpretation as belonging to a certain view or school of history?
- Is the historian writing with a particular purpose? Does this strengthen or weaken the interpretation?
- Is the interpretation adequately supported by a range of appropriate primary source material?
- Is this interpretation more or less convincing than other interpretations of the same issue?

■ Analysing and evaluating primary source material for the NEA

As emphasised on p. 32, your NEA is most of all an exercise in gauging how the value of the primary source material that you have selected for your essay would have contributed to the developing debate among historians over the issue in your question.

When testing the validity of the interpretations of your issue, you have been advised to consider each of the following questions:

■ What primary sources are available to the historian who is making a particular interpretation of the issue?
■ How would the historian be able to use such primary sources to help form their interpretation of the issue?

You have also been advised to make sure that you can identify a range of appropriate primary sources that would have enabled historians to support their particular interpretation. These primary sources then need to be thoroughly analysed and evaluated to demonstrate understanding of the ways in which they would have helped historians to create their particular interpretations of the issue.

Gathering primary sources — a reminder

Earlier in the guide (see p. 22) you were advised to select 6–8 primary sources to analyse and evaluate in your NEA and that these should cover a range of different types of material, such as:

■ official reports
■ diaries
■ letters
■ speeches
■ cartoons

■ newspaper reports
■ posters
■ pamphlets
■ photographs

Once you have gathered a range of suitable primary material, you can then analyse and evaluate this in order to test the validity of different interpretations of the issue you are studying.

Selecting credible sources

When you have identified a number of primary sources, you will need to assess their suitability for your NEA. The first area to consider when selecting your primary source material is its credibility.

Consider the following example. You have identified a school of thought that the main reason why the Civil Rights movement in the USA was successful was the leadership of Martin Luther King. In order to test the validity of this interpretation, you need to present and assess evidence from primary source material that supports it. Otherwise, the interpretation would be merely an opinion or an assertion. The evidence presented could include:

Tip

Remember to select 6–8 primary sources which represent a range of different types of evidence.

- examples of what King said
- examples of what King did
- what other people said or wrote about King at the time

In order to use this primary source material effectively you need to assess its credibility.

In making a judgement about the credibility of the evidence that you are going to present in your NEA, you should initially consider the following questions:

1 *What do you know about the author/creator of the source?* Is the author/creator an important figure in the Civil Rights movement? Has the author/creator got a reputation for honesty?

2 *How involved is the author/creator of the source?* Is she/he a neutral observer of the progress of the Civil Rights movement or has she/he got a vested interest in the role of Martin Luther King? This could lead to accusations of bias of some sort.

3 *Is the author/creator an eyewitness to events?* Eyewitness accounts of the role played by King are usually seen as more credible than second-hand evidence such as newspaper articles written by journalists, but is this really the case?

4 *Can the source you are intending to use be corroborated?* Have you got any more evidence to support the content or view of the particular source you are analysing? The volume of evidence can add strength to the argument.

5 *What is the wider context in which the source has been created?* Context refers to the circumstances in which the evidence has been created. This is particularly important when analysing historical sources as the author/creator may have been reacting with a range of emotions to the events or developments in relation to the Civil Rights movement, for example.

By asking these questions about the primary source material you have found, you should be in a position to select the most appropriate sources to evaluate as credible evidence for a historian making an interpretation.

Tip

Use these questions to begin to test the credibility of the primary sources that you have found.

Task 10

Judging credibility of evidence

Try to apply the five questions listed above to two of the primary sources that you have found for your NEA.

Alternatively, try to apply the questions to the following two pieces of primary source material. They are both contemporary newspaper accounts of the Peterloo Massacre which happened on 16 August 1819. It may be useful to look for some information about the authors of the two reports.

Source A

The events of yesterday will bring down upon the name of Henry Hunt and his accomplices, the deep and lasting curses of many a sorrowing family and of the sensible members of society at large. Having audaciously invited the attendance of a mass of people — which may be computed at 100,000 individuals — they proceeded to address them with language and suggestions of the usual desperate and malevolent character.

Just before two o'clock, the bugle sounded and the Manchester Yeomanry Cavalry advanced through the multitude and surrounded Hunt and his fellow orators upon the stage. Now comes a painful part of this article: the necessary ardour of the troops in the lawful execution of their duty has led, we lament to say, to some fatal and many serious incidents. A respectable innkeeper was run over and mortally wounded and another young man experienced the same fate.

From a report by Joseph Harrop, published in the local newspaper, the *Manchester Mercury* (17 August 1819)

Source B

The Manchester Yeomanry Cavalry rode into the crowd which gave way before them and eased their course to the stage where Hunt was speaking. Not a brick was thrown at them and not a pistol was fired during their advance. All was quiet and orderly, as if the cavalry had been the friends of the multitude and had advanced as such into the midst of them.

As soon as Hunt had been arrested and taken from the stage, a cry was made by the cavalry, 'Have at their flags.' In consequence the soldiers dashed not only at the flags on the stage but those that were posted among the crowd, riding most indiscriminately to the right and to the left in order to get at them. This set the people running in all directions and it was not until this act had been committed that any bricks were hurled at the military.

From that moment the Manchester Yeomanry Cavalry lost all command of temper. A person by the name of Saxton was standing by the stage. A private lunged at him with his sword and it was only by slipping aside that the blow cut into his coat and waistcoat. A man within five yards of us in another direction had his nose taken off completely by a blow from a sabre. Seeing all this hideous work going on, we felt an alarm which any man may be forgiven for feeling in a similar situation.

From a report by John Tyas, published in the national newspaper, *The Times* (19 August 1819)

Analysing and evaluating your chosen primary sources

Once you have determined the credibility of your chosen sources, you can begin to analyse and evaluate them in your answer. Remember that WJEC advises that you include the selected source directly in your answer. It is important that you are able to label your chosen sources with a full attribution.

This should contain the following aspects, if known:

- name of the author/creator
- role/position of the author/creator

- type of source
- name of source (if known)
- potential audience
- date of creation

Tip

Make sure that you label each source with a full attribution.

For example, 'Philip Gibbs, a journalist for the *Times* newspaper, in a report on preparations for the Somme offensive (3 July 1916)' is more effective than 'Philip Gibbs, a journalist, July 1916'.

Pitfalls to avoid

There are a number of pitfalls when dealing with primary sources. These include:

- Focusing *too much on the content* of the source, summarising or offering a précis of what it says or shows. Answers that do this are peppered with use of the phrase 'the source says…' or 'the source shows…'.
- Commentating on what the source is saying *in general terms* rather than focusing on what it is saying about the issue in the question. Try not to lose sight of the actual issue — analyse the content of the source for how it illustrates this particular issue.
- Making comments on the source *in isolation*. Analytical comments can be made about the source material but may fail to place the source in its proper historical context. What is happening around the time of the creation of the source is crucial to understanding the reaction of the creator.
- Making *formulaic and mechanical comments* on the authorship of the source. These include comments such as 'this account must be true because the author was there', 'the author is a politician and can't be trusted' or 'cartoons are of no use because they exaggerate features'.
- Failing to evaluate the source for its *usefulness in allowing a historian to make a particular interpretation*. Your sources should have been chosen because they are typical of the evidence base that a historian would have available, so part of the evaluation needs to contain a comment on how a historian making a particular interpretation would be able to use this source.

Tip

Avoid general, formulaic and mechanical comments when attempting to evaluate primary sources.

Having identified and selected the source material you are going to use and established its credibility, you can now begin to analyse and evaluate each source for its validity in helping to form and support different interpretations. You will need to consider most of the following aspects.

Considering the content of the source

This will allow you to consider the type of source — for instance, is it a letter or a cartoon? — and also what the source says or shows about the issue being studied. This can be done by focusing on key words, phrases or details in the source. For example, the source below contains lots of details concerning the Rebecca Riots but the actual information about the riots is quite straightforward.

A drawing of the Rebecca Riots, published in the *Illustrated London News* (1843)

Your use of this source should pick out a few obvious points illustrated, such as the violence of the protest and the attempt at disguise.

Considering the authorship of the source

This is sometimes called the origin of the source and should include consideration of what you can find out about the author or creator of the source. You will need to consider the role or position of the author/creator at the time that the source was created and the extent to which they would be in a position to know about the events or developments they are referring to.

For example, investigating and understanding the authorship is crucial to being able to analyse and evaluate the following source:

> People of Russia, our great and noble country is dying. Her end is near. Forced to speak openly, I, General Kornilov, declare that the Provisional Government, under extreme pressure from the Bolshevik majority in the Soviets, is killing the army and shaking the country until it bleeds. The terrible and awful conviction of the inevitable ruin of the country compels me in these frightful times to call upon all decent and patriotic Russians to save their dying land.

General Kornilov, in an appeal to the Russian people, published in the Petrograd newspaper, *Novoa Vremia* (August 1917)

Tip

Don't be tempted to describe or quote at length from the source — this is really copying.

Your evaluation of this source should include a clear indication that you know who General Kornilov is and why he has felt the need to issue such an appeal to people in Russia at this time.

Considering the perspective of the source

The perspective of the author is an important aspect to consider. If the author is a bystander or eyewitness, it is possible that he or she will be giving a factual account as they saw it. However, if the author is a figure with more involvement, you should consider their evidence from this perspective. The author may be a supporter or opponent of the government, regime or monarch they are commenting on. They may have a particular political, economic or religious view and this will be likely to have an impact on their outlook.

Another way of analysing the perspective of a source is to consider the language used. You might notice that, in many sources, some of the language used appears to be written in a particular way. The language may be extreme or exaggerated, either in a positive or a negative way. This can help you understand whether the author holds a particular perspective and can help you assess the validity of the evidence provided by the source.

Task 11

Perspective of a source

Read the following source and identify any 'loaded' words or phrases that suggest the source might be unreliable in its analysis of Oliver Cromwell. It would be certainly worth doing some research on the author and the audience when evaluating the source.

> Protector Cromwell has seized for himself despotic authority and the sovereignty of this realm under the mask of humility and public service. Obedience and submission of the people were never seen in England as at present. Cromwell has arrogantly crushed the spirit of the people so much that they dare not rebel. They can only murmur under their breath, though all live in eternal hope of a change of rule before long.

Lorenzo Paulucci, the Venetian ambassador to England, writing in a report for the Venetian authorities (21 February 1654)

Considering why the source was created

This involves investigating the purpose of the creation of the source and should also include consideration of the intended audience. For instance, was the source written to be published for a particular audience or was it in a private letter or a diary entry? A document written for a more public audience may be phrased differently from something written in a more private context. Some sources may have been written to inform, such as a report from a foreign correspondent in 1930s Germany. Another aspect to consider is whether the author was trying to win support for his or her cause, or was trying to persuade others to subscribe to a particular point of view.

Task 12

Purpose of a source

Consider the following source. What questions would you wish to ask of this source? Consider the author, the context and the audience.

> The population was pouring out of the city in long columns. On carts, on foot, on horseback. Everyone trying to save himself. All of them carrying away what they could. Exhaustion, dust, sweat, panic on every face, terrible dejection, pain and suffering. Their eyes are frightened, their movements furtive, ghastly terror oppresses them. It was as if the dust cloud that they stirred up had bound itself to them and could waft them away. I lie sleepless by the roadside and watch the infernal kaleidoscope. Even military vehicles are mixed up in it and across the fields march routed infantry and lost cavalry. Not a man among them still carries his full equipment. The exhausted throng pours down the valley, running and retreating.

Pal Kelemen, a Hungarian cavalry officer, writing in his diary about the fall of Lemberg in Poland (3 September 1914)

Considering the date of the source

The date of the source is crucial as this allows you to place the source in its proper historical context. Your NEA gives you an ideal opportunity to develop this particular skill. A particular source may say specific things, it will have a particular author, it will be written for a particular audience, but it is vital that you show understanding of the circumstances of the time when the source was actually created. The date that a source is written can have a considerable impact on its author, especially in influencing their view. The source may have been created just before or after a significant event or even during an event in the case of some photographs. When considering this aspect, a few well-chosen pieces of supporting material clearly linked to the source are much more effective than deploying lots of knowledge about the issue referred to in the source which is not really linked to its evaluation.

Consider the source that follows and the two responses below.

> Go to the alehouse of any enclosed country and there you will see the origin of poverty and poor rates. For whom are they to be sober? For whom are they to save their money? Such are the questions of the poor. If enclosures were beneficial to the poor, rates would not rise in these parishes after an act to enclose land. The poor in these parishes say 'Parliament may be looking after property but all I know is that I once had a cow and now an act of Parliament has taken it away from me.' I have heard thousands make similar speeches with truth.

Arthur Young, a writer on British agriculture, writing in his report, *An Enquiry into the Propriety of Applying Wastes* (1801)

Response 1: The source argues that the enclosure of land had had a terrible effect on the lives of many agricultural workers by 1801, leading to desperation and increased poverty due to the loss of common rights such as grazing cattle. There is certainly some truth in Young's writing as the loss of common rights included not just the right of cattle or sheep grazing, but also the grazing of geese, foraging for pigs, gleaning, berrying and fuel gathering. Moreover, Young's report is backed up by official statistics as by this time the movement of population from the countryside to the newly industrialising towns was increasing dramatically — London's population doubled between 1750 and 1801, for instance.

Response 2: The source says that poor people in the countryside had got much poorer because of enclosure and many of the people had turned to drinking to forget their problems. Approximately 4,000 parliamentary Acts of Enclosure were passed in this period, leaving virtually no common land. Although the enclosure of common land had been taking place since the time of the Tudors, advances in agriculture in the eighteenth century made consolidation of land profitable, inciting large-scale farmers and estate owners to claim more and more land. While commoners were compensated for their losses, they were generally given smaller and less arable parcels of land.

Response 1 uses evaluative phrases which link some contextual knowledge to the source. Examples are 'There is certainly some truth', which tries to justify Young's view, and use of the term 'Moreover', followed by a further example of contextual knowledge which corroborates the claims made by Young.

The second response contains more contextual knowledge but it is not used to evaluate the source. There are no evaluative words and the knowledge deployed does not explain whether the view in the source is valid or not.

> **Tip**
>
> Link your supporting material clearly to the source. This is more effective than deploying lots of knowledge about the general issue being discussed.

Task 13

Evaluating primary sources

In evaluating primary sources, it might be helpful to draw up a grid like the one below, so that you make sure you cover all the aspects that have been suggested.

Source	What does it say?	Who is the author?	Why was it written?	When was it written?	Link with a school of thought?	Judgement?
A						
B						
C						

How would a historian be able to use this source to support an interpretation?

As well as analysing your selected sources to demonstrate your ability for AO2, you must also consider *the value of the source material that you have selected in contributing to the developing debate among historians over the set issue.* In other words, how would a historian be able to use such primary sources to help form their interpretation of the issue?

This really is the crux of being able to analyse and evaluate primary sources for the NEA. It goes beyond what the source shows or means. It is about how the source might be used by a historian. What is its worth? How valuable is the evidence?

To consider the value of the primary source material effectively, you need to integrate your treatment of the sources with your discussion of the developing historical debate. This is not a difficult skill to master, but it does take the evaluation of the primary source material one stage further. Primary sources should not be evaluated in isolation. The key point is that historical interpretations cannot be deemed to be valid unless they are based on primary evidence. This is the very crux of your NEA.

Task 14

Linking a source with an interpretation

The source below was researched by a student looking to answer the following question:

'The most serious opposition to the Nazi party in the period 1933–45 came from religion.' How valid is this view of opposition to the Nazi party in this period?

> The tense times of 1938 with its repeated crises have demonstrated that just by crushing liberalistic and pacifist organizations these circles of opponents are not eliminated. The significance of liberalism does not lie in its organizational forms but in the inner attitude of the individuals carrying liberal ideas. In the intellectual circles of academia the liberalistic attitude predominated to this day and attempts to find among academic youth necessary recruits.
>
> In the field of art liberalistic influences have become stronger. The Museum at Breslau showed an exhibition of Chinese painting at the same time as the German Gymnastics and Sports Festival. Film and popular music lapse more and more into empty and erotic themes. More and more foreign books are seen in bookshops and democratically inclined teachers are still employed as educators. A teacher in Hanover had to be disciplined because he criticized our sports camps and community training courses. Leadership positions in the chambers of industry and commerce are mostly held by people who distance themselves from any commitment to the state. Indeed, business circles are responsible for the bulk of the criticism which is directed against the policies of the state.

From a surveillance report by the Sicherheitsdienst (SD), the intelligence agency of the SS (May 1938)

Consider the value of this source to a historian making an interpretation of this issue. What school of thought would be able to use this source as evidence for a particular interpretation?

Integration of your sources

At this stage in the process of your NEA, you should have gathered 6–8 primary sources which can be analysed and evaluated for their use in helping the different schools of thought to be developed. Now you will need to consider how your 6–8 primary sources can be integrated in this way.

Remember to consider how a historian would be able to use primary sources to help form their interpretation of the issue.

Task 15

Integration

Here are three examples of attempts at integration taken from NEA responses. Discuss whether each one has integrated the treatment of the primary source material with the discussion of the developing historical debate.

Example 1

'The Dissolution of the Monasteries occurred mainly because of the greed of Henry VIII.' How valid is this assessment of the reasons for the Dissolution of the Monasteries between 1536 and 1539?

> Manifest sin, vicious, carnal and abominable living, is daily used and committed amongst the little and small abbeys, priories and other such religious houses of monks, canons and nuns, where the congregation of such religious persons is under the number of 12 persons. The governors of such religious houses consume and waste the ornaments of their churches and their goods and chattels to the high displeasure of Almighty God, slander of good religion, and to the great infamy of the King's Highness and the realm. There can be no reformation of this problem unless such small houses are utterly suppressed and the religious persons in them committed to great and honourable monasteries where they may be compelled to live religiously for reformation of their lives.

Taken from the Act for the Dissolution of the Lesser Monasteries (1536)

This Act saw the closure of small monasteries that were worth less than £200 a year. Arguably this could be seen as a quick money-grabbing scheme that gave Henry short-term financial gain, possibly to fund a potential war against France and other Catholic powers. The source suggests a different explanation, claiming that the monks and nuns in these smaller religious houses were corrupt and so providing evidence for the interpretation that Henry dissolved the monasteries mainly for religious reasons.

Being an official document that was accepted by Parliament, one would naturally assume that the source is reliable, detailing the exact conditions of the smaller monasteries. There is the possibility that the information provided to Parliament (the basis on which they passed the Act in 1536) may have been edited to make the monasteries appear more inefficient than they were in reality.

This source in particular would be of great value to historians arguing that Henry was purely motivated by religious reform, such as David Loades in his book *Revolution in Religion: The English Reformation 1530–1570* published in 1992. On page 23 he states that 'Their wealth, and relative ease and security of the monastic life, had undermined their rigour' — therefore his stance on the topic is quite clear. It is often seen that Protestant historians are more ready to accept the view that religious houses were decaying, and it is Catholic historians who deny that claim and instead claim that Henry was tyrannical in his quest for further sources of income, including that of the monasteries. Since the Second World War religious persuasion has had less significance and there is a general agreement that Henry did want the money. Therefore, Loades is an example of an historian who does not conform to the general consensus regarding dissolution.

Example 2

'Lions led by donkeys.' How valid is this assessment of the British army on the Western Front during the First World War?

> We have not advanced 3 miles in the direct line at any point. We have only penetrated to that depth on a front of 8,000 to 10,000 yards. Penetration upon too narrow a front is quite useless for the purpose of breaking the line. In personnel the results of the operation have been disastrous; in terrain they have been absolutely barren: from every point of view the British offensive has been a great failure.

Winston Churchill, from a memorandum circulated to the cabinet (August 1916)

In this candid assessment of the early part of the Battle of the Somme, Churchill voices his criticism of the British offensive thus far in the war. He uses hyperbolic language to communicate his concern with the progress of the battle. This view is perhaps born from events which showed a complete neglect of infantry tactics and a persistence in making mistakes that cost lives. His tone is slighting in his belief that nothing has been achieved. His stating that the 'results of the operation have been disastrous' indicate that he feels this failure to be a result of strategy. His explicit criticism is a direct contrast to prevailing support for Haig at the time.

The extract is taken from a thorough analysis of the ground gained, the lack of strategic advantage in the territory obtained, the amount of munitions used, British casualties and the number of men fighting. His conclusion therefore, that the operation of the Somme was a 'great failure', is based on a detailed analysis of strategy. He corroborated his claims with a highly detailed breakdown of casualty statistics, which had clearly been provided by sources inside the War Office or GHQ in France. The War Committee dismissed the paper without giving it due discussion, preferring the statistics offered by General Robertson (Chief of the Imperial General Staff). He claimed, ludicrously, that the Germans had lost 300,000 men for every week of the battle — suggesting a total for the month exceeding one million men, a figure greater than the entire German army that was fighting at the Somme.

One has to approach this source with a degree of caution given that Churchill had requested command in the army in 1915 and had been refused by Haig. This source may, then, be fuelled by a bitter personal rivalry between Haig and Churchill. Given that the Battle of the Somme lasted until November 1916, his assessment of the offensive is not a whole one and is limited in this regard. An historian studying this would therefore have to take this into account. Churchill appears to possess the flexibility and strategical insight that arguably the generals lacked and foresaw the cost of continuing the battle. The source therefore gives an alternative perspective to the support for the Battle of the Somme at the time and provides a basis for later criticism to surface — which Churchill himself expanded on in his later assessment in 1939.

Example 3

Historians disagree about the reasons why the Civil Rights movement was a success. How far do you agree that the main reason why the Civil Rights movement was a success was the leadership of Martin Luther King?

> When the architects of our republic wrote the magnificent words of the Constitution and the Declaration of Independence...It is a dream deeply rooted in the American dream...I have a dream that one day this nation will rise up and live out the true meaning of its creed 'We hold these truths to be self-evident: that all men are created equal.' I have a dream that one day on the red hills of Georgia, sons of former slaves... I have a dream that one day in Alabama, with its vicious racists...let freedom ring from Stone Mountain of Georgia.

King's 'I have a dream' speech at the Lincoln Memorial in Washington (28 August 1963)

This source is a extract from a speech which touched the lives of black Americans who were going through a challenging time in American history but more importantly it brought middle-class white Americans into the circle of support which was vital for the Civil Rights movement to move forward. King speaks about 'the American dream' and he uses American sentiment and patriotism as he mentions the Constitution and the Declaration of Independence. The speech is powerful and is still spoken about due to his use of terms such as the Stone Mountain of Georgia where the Ku Klux Klan originated and where African Americans received a lot of the injustice that was given to them in this period.

The speech was so significant because of the great attention it brought from the media not just in America but around the world as well. To many historians this was the turning point in the Civil Rights movement because of the attention that it brought towards the injustice of treatment towards black Americans that was coming from the roots of the American government. The year has relevance and adds validity to the source as in the two years following the March on Washington the Civil Rights Act and Voting Rights Act were passed through Congress.

Using evaluative words and phrases

Both AO2 and AO3 expect you to be able to *evaluate*. Therefore evaluative words are crucial in assessing the value of primary source material in helping to create different interpretations and also in judging the validity of these interpretations. You may well have gathered a series of evaluative words and phrases during your course in preparation for your examinations. Such words and phrases will also be helpful when you evaluate both primary sources and different interpretations in your NEA.

The following phrases might be helpful when making evaluations of your material.

Primary source material (AO2)

The view in Source A is supported by…

The view in Source B is challenged by…

This view in Source C can be illustrated by pointing out that…

There is little evidence to support the view in Source D.

Different interpretations (AO3)

The interpretation as expressed by this group of historians is valid because…

The interpretation as expressed by X is questionable because…

This particular interpretation can be criticised because…

Historians such as X give too much significance to…

This particular interpretation is not supported by valid and reliable evidence.

> **Tip**
>
> Remember to use evaluative words and phrases when considering the worth of primary sources.

Summary

Here is a basic checklist of the types of question that you can use to analyse and evaluate the primary source material that you have gathered:

- What type of source is it?
- What does the source say about the issue?
- Who created the source?
- What do we know about the author/creator?
- Is the author/creator trustworthy?
- Why was the source created?
- Who was the intended audience?
- When was the source created?
- What was happening at the time of the creation of the source?
- Can the source be corroborated?
- How would a historian be able to use this source to support their interpretation?

■ From draft to finished product

By this stage in the process of your NEA you should have done the following:

- Written a draft introduction — possibly giving an answer in a nutshell.
- Gained an awareness of the historical debate over the issue in your question — with at least two different interpretations or schools of thought identified.
- Gathered 6–8 primary sources which can be analysed and evaluated for their use in helping the different schools of thought to be developed.
- Constructed a diagram or a chart which outlines the key areas to discuss. Such a chart was advised on p. 20 to give you the structure and outline that you need before you start writing your essay. This will be invaluable in helping you write up your answer.

Task 16

Updating planning

You could now update your planning chart so it follows the line taken by your enquiry. One suggestion is given below.

Introduction	Answer in a nutshell
Summary of the developing historical debate	Avoid a narrative — make this a short précis
Consideration of the validity of Interpretation 1	Evaluate the significance of the evidence base
Consideration of the validity of Interpretation 2	Evaluate the significance of the evidence base
Conclusion/judgement	Make sure this flows logically from the parts above

Having done this you are now in a position to be able to begin writing up your work. Bear in mind the following points, most of which have been emphasised already in the guide.

- Keep your focus on the actual question set. Refer back to the question on regular occasions to ensure that you don't lose this focus.
- Avoid description and waffle — this shows drift and lack of focus.
- Ensure that you are aware of at least two different interpretations or schools of history.
- Make sure that you have a range of 6–8 primary sources.
- Make sure that in your evaluation of the primary sources you are considering how important they are as part of the evidence base for creating an interpretation.
- Your conclusion or judgement should follow from what you have said in your introduction and in the main body of your answer.

Tip

The more research and reading that you have done around the issues raised in your question, the more straightforward the writing up will be.

The style of your essay

As advised on p. 9, your NEA should be presented as a holistic essay that integrates the qualities expected in the three assessment objectives (AOs) in a sustained and sophisticated manner. However, many students still produce essays that separate their work into sections, which deal with each AO in isolation. Typically this will involve:

- Part 1 — an introduction (AO1)
- Part 2 — an evaluation of 6–8 sources (AO2)
- Part 3 — a description of the writings of different historians on the topic (AO3)
- Part 4 — a conclusion (AO1)

Students will sometimes use subtitles to introduce these different sections. *Please try to avoid this approach.* It is vital to note that assessors — both your teacher and WJEC moderators — have been guided to give greater credit to essays which integrate the demands of the three assessment objectives than to essays which are written in sections. An integrated answer shows linkage between the component parts of the answer. This includes linking the evaluation of primary source material to the formation of varying interpretations.

Task 17

Linking source evaluation with interpretations

Can you spot how this is approached in the paragraph below?

The 1960s saw the development of various fresh interpretations of the reasons for the outbreak of the Bolshevik revolution, which can be classed as revisionist in tone. One of these interpretations argues that the success of revolution was less to do with Lenin's leadership and more to do with the underlying instability of the government which encouraged the growth of revolutionary sentiment. This particular interpretation can be based on a wide range of primary evidence such as the appeal made by General Kerensky in August 1917.

An integrated answer also includes linking the evaluation of primary sources to the development of the historical debate.

Task 18

Linking source evaluation with the development of the historical debate

Can you spot how this is tackled in the paragraph below?

Clearly, close scrutiny of this source demonstrates it to be vital first-hand evidence from a renowned and highly-praised general writing during the conflict. Historians writing immediately after the conclusion of the war would have been able to use this source and other similar material to develop and support their interpretation of the conduct of the British generals as both inspiring and wise. Examples of this early group of historians include J.H. Boraston and G.A.B. Dewar writing in 1919 in their book *Sir Douglas Haig's Dispatches*. The historians were able to use sources such as these to represent Haig's strong leadership and this backed up the public perception of him and generals as war heroes. Historians writing in the immediate postwar period would not have made the interpretation that lions were led by donkeys. This could have been largely due to the postwar euphoria and the extent of patriotic views that prevailed at this time.

Reaching a conclusion

This part of your answer needs to come last. This should be of little surprise as it is really a summary of the arguments and interim judgements that you have laid out in your answer.

You are asked to respond to a question, so the conclusion is a final judgement on the question set.

For example, your question will not have been *'What were the causes of the French Revolution of 1789?'* but rather *'Financial problems were the main cause of the French Revolution of 1789.' How valid is this view of the causes of the French Revolution?*

The question mark at the end of the question invites an answer — a judgement in the conclusion. Any interim judgements that you have made on the validity of different interpretations as you have been drafting your notes and writing up your essay should lead to an overall judgement based on the critical use you have made of the evidence.

In the example question above, you would need to make judgements throughout your answer about the relative importance of varying causes of the French Revolution and how this has been reflected by different historians. The conclusion will then allow you to bring together all your interim judgements to give an overall answer to the question set.

Tip

Avoid presenting your NEA work in discrete sections: the better-rewarded answers will approach the enquiry in a holistic and integrated manner.

Task 19

Concluding your answer

Here are three examples of conclusions to NEA questions. How effective do you consider these to be? Look out for:

- reference to the actual question set — can you tell what the question is from the conclusion?
- drifting into description
- reference to at least two different interpretations or schools of history
- reference to the evidence base for creating an interpretation
- an answer to the question set

Conclusion 1

'Parliament was more responsible for the outbreak of the Civil War than the King.' How valid is this assessment of the outbreak of civil war by 1642?

In conclusion the revisionist interpretation is most valid as it states that the Civil War was caused by the ineptitude of the King to govern effectively three different kingdoms, especially when unsupported by a divisive Parliament unwilling to help. Therefore, both King and Parliament were responsible for the outbreak of war due to their inability to co-operate and work in a symbiotic relationship. Both the Whig and later Marxist interpretations rely on structuralist explanations whereby the Civil War was inevitable and exacerbated by a tyrannical king whose power needed to be challenged and distributed. However, scrutiny of the available evidence from the time — most of which is heavily biased to one side or another — would suggest that the most valid interpretation is that Charles was a poor monarch and politician with none of his father's political shrewdness or flexibility whose intentions to modernise and unite the church and state across the British Isles were well intentioned but poorly planned and implemented. Existing structural weaknesses in the economy and in the Church were made worse by Charles' poor diplomacy and also by Parliament's lack of willingness in trying to remedy or repair those weaknesses. Therefore it was the inability of the Crown and Parliament to co-operate which led to the outbreak of civil war and the overthrowing of the old monarchical system.

Conclusion 2

How far do you agree that the USA was unsuccessful in the Vietnam War mainly because the government lost the trust of the American public?

To conclude, the interpretation that the USA was unsuccessful in the Vietnam War mainly because the government lost the trust of the American public is agreeable to a small extent, because although a loss of trust in the government did occur, it did not stop the US government from continuing the war. As shown through the sources used, it is clear that Summers' interpretation is the most valid due to its sophisticated reasoning on why the USA had lost the war with Vietnam, as a lack of politico-military assessment was put forward by American political leaders. The ineffective tactics used in order to fight the Vietcong which portrayed the Vietcong's strength that dominates Kolko's interpretation further demonstrates this. This contributes to Summers' interpretation as being most valid as to why the USA lost the war, thus disputing the interpretation in the question.

Conclusion 3

Do you agree with the view that Robert Peel was the most effective political leader in the period 1834 to 1880?

In conclusion, Peel was an effective political party leader until he became prime minister as his priority became the state rather than his party. During the early 1830s the Tory Party had collapsed, partly due to Catholic Emancipation and partly due to the party's attitude towards parliamentary reform. It was however under Peel's leadership that the Tory Party was able to naturally revive itself. In August 1841 the newly named Conservative Party won a substantial electoral majority in the general election, making Peel the prime minister 1841–46. Up until this point Peel was said to be one of the most effective political leaders for decades. However, during these years, Peel faced several problems consisting of economic hardship, abysmal working conditions, criticism from Ireland and pressure to repeal the Corn Laws. Peel was said by some historians to be a capable leader who was unable to adjust to the post-1832 world. As a leader, Disraeli was outstanding and his ideas have proved timeless as they remain useful, applicable and approachable over a century later. Gladstone by contrast was a character of his era. He was often correct but his ruminations on free trade and Irish Home Rule do not map well to modern political and economic situations. Peel was believed to set the foundation for following leaders of this time. Without the founder of modern Conservatism who first led Britain to stability and prosperity, the leaders who followed would have not been as effective or successful.

Presenting your NEA

Remember that the NEA is an extended essay and therefore requires continuous prose. It will need to flow as a piece of writing and, where possible, avoid the use of bullet points and subheadings.

There are no specific marks available for the quality of English, but as you have the chance to use a spell checker do take advantage of it, and do check for typos and misspellings. This is often called proofreading. Be critical of your writing style, look out for both grammatical and spelling errors, and make sure that *all* research information that you use has been properly referenced.

You must also produce your NEA in a clear and readable font, such as Arial 12, and include page numbers on each page. You should also include your name and examination number on each page in a header.

Word count

WJEC recommends that NEA essays are between 3,000 and 4,000 words. This word limit is for your benefit. If you write less than the guidance advises then it is unlikely that you are dealing with the topic in sufficient depth. If you write more — and in many cases this is very tempting — then this usually shows a tendency for you to either describe developments or events in greater depth or to repeat points already made, rather than focusing on the key skills of analysis and judgement. The skills that you need to demonstrate can be shown effectively within the word limit.

As overlong responses are often descriptive and repetitive, the marking guidance is that such responses should be restricted to Band 5 marks because they would not meet the criteria for Band 6, which rewards essays that are 'coherent, lucid, concise and well-constructed'. Exceeding the word limit will cost you marks.

Referencing

WJEC advises that you include your selected sources and any extracts directly into your answer, rather than in an appendix. Therefore referencing is essential, especially where sources and extracts are utilised. It allows you to:

- acknowledge the work of other writers
- show the origin of your sources easily
- distinguish your ideas from the ideas that you have discovered in your research
- acknowledge where you got your information from and not try to claim for yourself ideas and opinions that you have taken from others

WJEC does not stipulate any particular form of referencing but the two that are most commonly seen are author–date style and footnotes. Both of these give you the opportunity to insert citations into your NEA and to reference your sources.

Author–date style

WJEC recommends strongly that you place the actual primary sources that you use, and any extracts that you deem appropriate, into the account itself. They are easier to read in this way and can be easily referenced using author–date style. In this style the references are placed in the account itself, not in footnotes. Brackets are used for this

Tip

Your conclusion allows you to bring together your interim judgements to give an overall answer to the question set.

Tip

Be rigorous in your proofreading. Is your work free of typos and grammar errors? Does your work read well and make sense?

Tip

Make your words count: don't lose focus and drift away from the question set. More words do not mean a better answer.

purpose, giving information about the author or creator of the source or extract and the date of publication. In this style, the inclusion of additional information is not as common as in the use of footnotes. Here are two examples:

[A Nazi propaganda poster encouraging popular use of the radio (1937)]

[Leon Trotsky, in a speech made at an emergency session of the Petrograd Soviet (24 October 1917)]

Footnotes

One other common style of referencing is footnote style. Footnotes are often seen when sources or extracts are referred to more briefly or where the work of a particular historian is referred to. In this style, any reference information is given in footnotes at the foot of each page rather than in the body of the text. Footnotes should be numbered in one sequence throughout your report. When you insert a footnote, add a number in the text and create a corresponding footnote at the bottom of the page.

Here is an example:

This comical mockery of wartime leadership adds strength to Clark's interpretation that the generals were 'grossly incompetent'[1] as it highlights the disconnection that the generals had from the front line. Nevertheless the anti-establishment feeling of the time alongside the fact that traditionalist historians were emotionally connected to the war weakens their argument, as they seem to want to blame someone for the high casualties on the Western Front: in this case, the generals.

[1]Taken from *The Donkeys* by Alan Clark, published in 1961.

Footnotes are properly used to identify the origin of the sources or extracts. However, be careful with footnotes that you do not use them to add extra information. If the information is deemed important, then it should be in the essay. If the footnotes contain such extra information, it should be included in the word count.

Be careful about using unreferenced assertions as these are not acceptable in NEAs. It is worth using phrases like 'It seems reasonable to suggest that…' or 'One possible explanation is…', always making sure that you include appropriate references to the historians or contemporaries who may have put forward these suggestions or explanations. Avoid generalisations and broad statements such as 'It is widely believed that…' or 'German historians argue that…', with no direct references to support such claims.

Using a bibliography

At the end of your NEA you must include a bibliography. You will have used a referencing system such as those mentioned above to identify primary source materials and extracts. These should also be included in a bibliography, which is an indication of any material from which you have taken information. Typically, in your bibliography you should look to list books, articles or websites that you have used in your research.

Ensure that your bibliography contains the name of the book or article, the author and the date of publication.

Tip

Make sure that you include the sources and extracts that you use in the body of the account. This is clearer than placing them in an appendix.

Tip

It is a good idea to create a bibliography as you go along because it is a record of all the material that you have read in order to complete your NEA. This can also show you whether you have consulted a range of different materials in your research, or whether you have relied too heavily on one type of material, such as websites.

Summary

- Your essay should be word processed.
- It should be completed in 3,000–4,000 of your own words (excluding primary sources and extracts).
- Primary sources and extracts used must be clearly referenced and inserted into the essay in the appropriate part of the response.
- Every page of your response should be numbered in a header which includes your centre number and your name and number.
- A word count must be provided.
- References/footnotes and a bibliography must be included.

■ Reviewing your work — formal and specific

Once the NEA is in progress, your teacher can review the progress of your work and provide you with oral and written advice on aspects of your work at a general level. This can be done in lesson time or in less formal sessions. Having been provided with such advice at a general level, you are allowed to revise and redraft aspects of your work. You should expect to produce several versions of your NEA before you will feel relatively confident about it in draft form.

Once the draft of your NEA is completed, you will have the opportunity to discuss it with your teacher on a more formal basis. WJEC calls this process one of *Formal Review*.

At the Formal Review, it is expected that your teacher will review your whole draft NEA work with you, with particular reference to the assessment objective criteria as outlined in the NEA mark scheme. This will enable you to reflect and to take the initiative in making your own amendments to your work. It is best for this review to be carried out once a full first draft of your work has been completed.

Following the Formal Review, a form is completed by you — not your teacher — recording the nature of the advice given. This form must be included with your completed NEA work when it is submitted for assessment.

Discussion about your completed draft work during a Formal Review session should be at a general level with no attempt to correct errors, point out omissions or misunderstandings or improve your grammar or presentation.

The Formal Review form can be obtained from the WJEC website. Here is a copy of part of a Formal Review form with a record of the advice given, completed by a learner.

Assessment	Points noted by the LEARNER as discussed at the Formal Review relating to the assessment criteria
AO1	I was advised that my draft showed clear understanding of the key issue stated in my question. The conclusion offered a judgement which backed up the arguments I used in the answer.
	I was advised that my introduction needed to be more focused on the specific enquiry and this was an area that needed attention in the final submission.
AO2	While my analysis and evaluation of the selected sources was generally good I was advised to:
	–present a wider range of primary sources
	–research the historical context more clearly
	–link the evaluation of the primary sources more obviously to the forming of different schools of thought
AO3	My teacher was disappointed here as there was little evidence that I had gone beyond a summary of historians' views over civil rights.
	I was advised to use my chosen primary sources to show how different historians use evidence to support their interpretations.
Signed (Staff)	
Signed (Learner)	

Normally, one Formal Review will be sufficient to enable you to further understand and discuss the demands of the assessment, but if there is a need for another Formal Review, then another review and form can be completed.

It is important to understand the difference between 'general advice' and 'specific advice'. If the advice given to you is 'general advice' (which is advice referring to demonstrating the criteria for the AOs as laid down in the mark scheme) then it does not need to be recorded regularly, but only in the Formal Review. However, it is possible that, for some students, more specific advice is occasionally needed. Any advice to you which goes beyond pointing out the assessment criteria in the mark scheme is considered to be 'specific advice'.

Specific advice is defined as any advice which encourages or advises the student to amend, change or improve any aspect of their response. Examples include the following:

- Having reviewed your work, you are given advice and suggestions as to how the work may be altered in order to meet the assessment criteria.
- You are given indications of errors or omissions that leave you with no opportunity for individual initiative.
- You are provided with writing frames specific to your NEA task (e.g. outlines, paragraph headings or section headings).
- You are directed to use certain sources and extracts to alter your work on the development of the historical debate.

If any advice given to you is defined as 'specific advice' then it *must* be recorded on the Specific Advice form and be taken into account in the final mark awarded to the essay. Your teacher will not award Band 6 marks to any candidate who has been given specific advice to amend, change or improve any aspect of their response during the completion of their essay.

Tip

The Formal Review form is completed by you. It shows the general feedback given by your teacher about your draft work.

Tip

If you are struggling with some of the demands of the NEA then accepting specific advice can be very helpful.

The Specific Advice form can be obtained from the WJEC website. Here is a copy of part of a Specific Advice form with a record of the advice given, completed by a learner.

Please note below any specific advice given in relation to each of the Assessment Objectives or any further advice with regard to the NEA. Further information about the nature of the advice that can be given can be found in the Teacher Guide for Unit 5 and in the JCQ *Instructions for conducting coursework*.

Assessment	Points noted by the LEARNER as discussed at meetings where specific advice was given
AO1	*My teacher was not satisfied with the structure of my work. It was messy and difficult to follow. I was given advice on how to structure my work using a basic writing model.*
AO2	*I had a range of primary sources and I had tried to evaluate these for their help to historians. However, there was a need for a greater range. My teacher directed me to two collections of sources which would allow me to choose a greater range.*
AO3	*My teacher was quite happy with my understanding of the historical debate over the monasteries. With better links I should get a good mark for AO3.*
Any other advice	*I was given two weeks to submit another draft to see if I had acted on the specific advice given.*
Signed (Staff)	
Signed (Learner)	

A learner log

It is recommended that you keep a learner log as you progress with your NEA work. The use of such a log is not compulsory and the log will not be worth any marks, but it will be very useful in several ways:

- To help you to keep a record of your progress and of your sources. You will need to reference the materials you have used and the learner log can help to record them.
- To help with recording — you may have a brainwave or excellent thought but then forget it because you did not write it down. Use of the learner log can help if this happens.
- To help your teacher see the progress you have made.
- To provide evidence that the NEA is your own work.

A completed example is shown below.

Candidates undertaking the NEA are required to keep a detailed record of their own research, planning and the resources consulted. Resources are defined as books, websites and audio/visual resources. In addition, if those resources are used, then they must be referenced. This record may be required by the WJEC but does not have to be submitted with the NEA. Candidates are advised to keep this record securely until after the end of the examination series with any 'rough notes and materials as evidence of work done independently' as required by the NEA regulations.
Use the checklist below to indicate where the requirements of the log have been met.

Tip

The learner log is not compulsory but can be a useful tool to keep track of your progress while tackling your NEA.

Content of the log	Yes	No
This log includes a brief account of the planning of the NEA	✓	
This log includes a brief account of the research undertaken	✓	
This log includes a brief account of the resources consulted	✓	
Details of referencing: You are required to ensure that if you use the same wording as a published work you place quotation marks around the passage and state where it came from.		
This log includes referencing of the resources used in the NEA	✓	
Details of planning: You are required to include details of planning though these do not have to be extensive. Further details may be provided on an additional attached sheet.		
During the course of the extended essay I have continually planned and created new drafts and rewritten sections to include a better balance of content, source evaluation and discussion of debates. I felt I favoured content too heavily in my first drafts. I also revised the structure of my argument, including more counter-arguments to fully debate the issue in the question.		
Details of research undertaken: You are required to include details of the research undertaken — such as general resources studied, document packs consulted or visits to sites. Further details may be provided on an additional attached sheet.		
I visited various websites connected with the generals on the Western Front, Haig in particular. I consulted both books and internet articles which provided varying interpretations of the generals and their conduct. I studied the major schools of thought over the issue and gathered primary sources on the issue. Here I made use of the library in the English Department in college which had a considerable amount of war literature in both prose and poetry. I also studied a number of television documentaries about the Somme and the role played by the generals.		
Details of resources consulted: You are required to include a bibliography at the end of your work for the NEA. Any other resources consulted may be included below or may be provided on an additional attached sheet. These details should be provided as in these examples: (a) for books and journals: Morrison, A: 'Mary, Queen of Scots'; Weston Press (2002) (b) for websites: http://hwb.wales.gov.uk/Resources		
Books: *Terraine, J: The Smoke and the Fire: Myths and Anti-myths of War, 1861–1945; Pen & Sword Books (1980)* *Laffin, J: British Butchers and Bunglers of World War I; The History Press (2003)* *Keegan, J: The First World War; Vintage (2000)* *Walter, G (ed): The Penguin Book of First World War Poetry; Penguin (2006)* **Websites:** *http://www.bbc.co.uk/guides/zq2y87h* *https://www.telegraph.co.uk/history/world-war-one/inside-first-world-war/part-two/10352633/first-world-war-generals.html* *https://yougov.co.uk/topics/politics/articles-reports/2014/01/09/wwi-generals-let-down-troops* *https://www.historyextra.com/period/first-world-war/british-generals-infighting-lost-battle-of-the-somme/* *https://www.warmuseum.ca/firstworldwar/history/people/generals/sir-douglas-haig/* **Videos:** *https://www.youtube.com/watch?v=VOCwqA-UB-0* *https://www.youtube.com/watch?v=sMoKIWX4IM0*		

A final checklist

Your teacher will be looking for the aspects listed in the following task when assessing your answer. You may also find this useful as a checklist.

Task 20

The final check

Can you answer yes to all these points in relation to your NEA? They all relate to the AOs that you will be assessed against.

- Is the knowledge shown accurate?
- Is your answer lucid and coherent?
- Is your answer addressing the question set?
- Is there analysis and evaluation of a range of 6–8 primary/contemporary sources?
- Have you attempted to evaluate the selected primary/contemporary sources in order to test the validity of the interpretation contained in the question?
- Have you attempted to focus the analysis of these sources on addressing how and why the interpretation may have been formed?
- Is there a valid discussion of the historiography surrounding the issue in the question — that is, is there a sound understanding of the developing historical debate?

Summary

- Ask for and accept general advice from your teacher regularly.
- If you are struggling with any aspects of the NEA, don't be cautious about asking for specific advice on how to manage these challenges.

- The NEA will help develop many transferable study skills — use of a learner log can be effective in recording your progress.

▮A completed example

Here is an example of a completed NEA. It includes some examiner comments to demonstrate the extent to which the essay fulfils the assessment criteria.

Historians disagree about the reasons why the Civil Rights movement was a success. How far do you agree that the main reason why the Civil Rights movement was a success in the 1960s was the leadership of Martin Luther King?

The question gives the opportunity to offer a substantiated judgement — note the use of the phrase 'the main reason' — and invites analysis of a major historical debate — the reasons for the success of the Civil Rights movement in the 1960s.

Martin Luther King was instrumental in the success of the Civil Rights movement. His peaceful protests and powerful speeches gained mass publicity worldwide and his belief in non-violent methods to achieve equality came from what he saw of Gandhi and what he did over the British Empire. King's role was hugely significant for the African-American equality movement from the acts of the Bus Boycotts in the mid-1950s until his death in 1968. His Nobel Prize award in 1964 came from his influential speeches such as the March to Washington the previous year and the passing of the Voting Act and Civil Rights Act while Johnson was President.

There is a hint of an answer in the first sentence but it could be much more focused on the actual question. Note the drift away from 'success' to 'significance'. They are linked but they are not the same historical concepts.

While King was massively important in the Civil Rights movement and is considered the main reason for the success by historians, there are many other factors that have to be taken into account for the many victories that were gained by other key figures. This essay will argue against the question of King's leadership being the main reason for success in the Civil Rights movement. Lyndon B. Johnson, Malcolm X and many other groups have to be taken into account for their great work that helped black Americans achieve equality when there was nothing. Laws were passed and respect was gained due to the impressive work that they put in during the 1960s.

This is a more focused paragraph which attempts to give an answer 'in a nutshell'. There is a reference to 'historians' which hopefully will set up the opportunity to look at the developing historical debate about the success of the Civil Rights movement in the 1960s.

In the summer of 1963, 200,000 men and women gathered in Washington to listen to a man who is widely considered the most significant factor of the Civil Rights movement. On 28 August he made his 'I have a dream' speech which brought worldwide attention to Martin Luther King himself and also the violence and injustice on black Americans through the media.

A completed example

No attempt is made to link this paragraph with the introduction and 'answer in a nutshell'. A simple linking mechanism could be a reference to King's leadership as shown by his oratory. The lack of linking sentences is a weakness shown throughout the essay.

> **SOURCE 1**
>
> **When the architects of our republic wrote the magnificent words of the Constitution and the Declaration of Independence...It is a dream deeply rooted in the American dream. I have a dream that one day this nation will rise up, live out the true meaning of its creed — 'we hold these truths to be self-evident: that all men are created equal.' I have a dream that one day on the red hills of Georgia, sons of former slaves...I have a dream that some day in Alabama, with its vicious racists...but not only that, let freedom ring from Stone Mountain of Georgia.**
>
> [Martin Luther King's.'I have a dream' speech at the Lincoln Memorial on 28 August 1963 in Washington]

Source 1 is an extract from his speech which touched the lives of black Americans who were going through a challenging time in American history but more importantly it brought the middle class white Americans into the circle of support which was vital for the Civil Rights movement to move forward. King used American sentiment to say to white Americans that there was no difference in how they felt about America; he uses patriotism as he mentions 'the Constitution and the Declaration of Independence' which Americans feel extremely strongly about, especially the white middle class. Again, using that sentiment as King speaks about 'the American dream' and even if you weren't part of the 200,000 supporters in Washington on that day support gained through the TV came from such an emotive speech. Although it did bring support from a very important group in the white middle class, this was however, a negative development for some supporters as he was perceived by black nationalists as just wanting equality and not having the same outlook on the black movement as being superior as other significant figures. The speech is powerful and still spoken about due to the use of terms of black American feeling such as the mentioning of Stone Mountain of Georgia where the Ku Klux Klan originated and where African Americans received a lot of the injustice that was given to them during this period. The speech shows that although he wanted equality, he didn't want anything more than that and this was the downside of King's approach to the Civil Rights movement unlike Malcolm X, the Black Panthers and many other more rebellious figures who wanted more than equality and wanted blacks to thrive.

The speech was so significant because of the great attention that it brought from the media, not just in America but around the world as well and if the name of King wasn't known already, it was now. The speech put him in the limelight due to its powerful nature; to many historians it was the turning point for King and the Civil Rights movement because of the attention that it brought towards

> the treatment of injustice towards black Americans that was coming from the roots of the American government. The location of the speech has great relevance to how powerful the speech was because as King stood at the steps of the Lincoln Memorial, he discussed problems that were still occurring 100 years after President Lincoln had abolished slavery by issuing the Emancipation Proclamation. Again King uses American feelings to grab their attention and he did this by using a significant figure who could be perceived to have started the freedom of African Americans.

The source is a decent choice, but the use of various phrases is confusing. Also, there is no attempt to introduce the source by explaining why it has been chosen — presumably to reflect the quality of King as an inspirational speaker. Again the failure to introduce and integrate source material is a weakness shown throughout the essay.

This section is a basic analysis of the content and the impact of the particular speech. While relevant points are made, there is no attempt to evaluate the source in its historical context — the circumstances in 1963 which led to King showing his leadership qualities in rallies like this. There is also no attempt to link evidence of this kind to the forming of and support for particular schools of thought over the success of the Civil Rights movement.

> However, you could say that this was a turning point in the Civil Rights movement, without the help of Lyndon B. Johnson who passed the Acts that King protested for, his campaign would have meant nothing other than a show of resistance against the injustice in America.

A different historical concept — 'turning points' — is referred to here and there is also a reference to Johnson. This is an attempt to give some balance to the answer but it is not really successful.

> The source is high in value as it shows how Martin Luther King used his powerful speeches to succeed in the Civil Rights movement and this backs up my own knowledge and understanding of how King was great in using feelings and emotions to gain support from black Americans during the 1950s and 1960s. The year has relevance and adds validity to the source as in the two years following the March in Washington the Civil Rights Act and the Voting Rights Act were passed through Congress and this implies the impact that King had during the Civil Rights movement in America.

A judgement is given on the value of the source but this is not linked to the particular enquiry about King's leadership or to the formation of any particular school of thought over the reasons for the success of the Civil Rights movement.

Note the reference to 'this backs up my own knowledge and understanding'. This phrase will appear several times in the essay but is not needed as it doesn't add anything to the answer.

A completed example

> To many Americans King was like family and was greatly important to them because of the Civil Rights movement and how he was as a human. His eulogy after his death from Benjamin Mays shows how valuable he was to the movement. It was no surprise that Mays would be the only speaker at King's funeral, a man who King once described as 'my intellectual father'.

Again note the lack of a linking mechanism. A good way to tackle this would be to use a linking phrase like 'another example of the effective leadership of King was his policy of non-violence'.

> **SOURCE 2**
>
> **To be honoured by being requested to give the eulogy at the funeral of Dr Martin Luther King Jr is like asking one to eulogize his deceased son. Here was a man who believed with all of his might that the pursuit of violence at any time is ethically and morally wrong. No reasonable person would deny that the activities and the personality of Dr King contributed largely to the success of the student sit-in movements in abolishing segregation in downtown establishments and that his activities contributed mightily to the passage of the Civil Rights legislation of 1964 and 1965.**
>
> [Benjamin Mays' eulogy at Martin Luther King's funeral, 9 April 1968]

Some would consider Mays' eulogy to be a reflection on King's life and therefore not a primary source. However, as the question invites discussion of the Civil Rights movement in the 1960s, this would be deemed to be a primary source.

> Within this source, Mays speaks about King as his son due to being a teacher of King throughout his Morehouse College years; he would often listen to Mays preach at the chapel. Mays had a great influence on King due to his belief in non-violent methods to gain achievements. King referred to Mays as his 'spiritual and intellectual mentor' and all the way through the eulogy he speaks about the great beliefs that King applied to his methods that made him the great figure in the Civil Rights movement. Mays mentions the passing of the Civil Rights legislation in 1964 and 1965; this backs up my own knowledge and understanding of how Martin Luther King was instrumental in achieving these acts which black Americans were fighting for.
>
> The source has great utility as it shows how powerful King was in the movement as he is spoken about with such strong words. It validates why he is even questioned as the main reason for the success. Mays backs up my own knowledge and understanding as he mentions the passage of legislation during the 1960s which proved to be greatly substantial in the progression of equality for black Americans. In Mays' eulogy he also mentions how King's approach to the discrimination in America during the 1950s and 1960s contributed to the student following which also proved to be instrumental from my own knowledge of the subject.

These aruguments increase the usefulness of the source as it backs up the question of King's leadership being the main reason for success.

The source could be perceived to be biased because the speech is at a funeral of the key figure in question: even though Mays was a great friend and tutor to King, he has to be respectful on such an awful day for many people. A eulogy has to show the deceased in a good light and although many peers of King would say that he and his methods were great, there is evidence to show that the non-violent approach wasn't always the top way to gain these acts.

Some valid comments are made here on the source's provenance and its context.

This source's value to a historian is high in value due to how Mays talks about King with such powerful words proving that this work meant so much to people around America and the world. It justifies why King is considered to be the main reason for the success of the Civil Rights movement but as it is a speech at his funeral, there is a high basis of bias towards the man in question so the credibility of the source has to be questioned.

Again a judgement is given on the value of the source and a tantalising reference to historians is made but this is as far as it goes. The judgement given here is linked to the particular enquiry about King and Civil Rights but not to the formation of any particular school of thought over the reasons for the success of the Civil Rights movement.

The significant contribution of Martin Luther King is shown in him being awarded the Nobel Peace Prize for his participation and significant leadership in the Civil Rights movement and in 1986 America dedicated a federal holiday to him.

Again, a linking sentence would help: for example, 'Further evidence regarding the leadership of King can be seen by…'.

SOURCE 3

He is the first person in the western world to have shown us that a struggle can be waged without violence. Today we pay tribute to Martin Luther King, the man who has never abandoned his faith in the unarmed struggle he is waging, who has suffered for his faith, whose life and the lives of his family have been threatened and who nevertheless has never faltered.

[Martin Luther King's citation at the Nobel Peace Prize awards, 1964]

A good choice of source which shows another facet of King's leadership — his steadfastness.

A completed example

> Winning a Nobel Peace Prize shows how influential King was in the movement against the unfair treatment of African Americans and this is supported by the fact that in 1964 King helped pass the Voting Rights Act. Subsequently Source 3 shows the progression that the Civil Rights movement was making with King at the forefront of the leadership team.

Note the drift again here. King's 'influence' is cited but then the essay does drift back to refer to his 'leadership'.

> Although the source supports why King was the main reason for the progression of the Civil Rights movement, it could be interpreted as biased similarly to the eulogy. King is the main person that the source is about and at such a prestigious event the speaker will only speak great and meaningful words. The author of this citation would not want to damage King's reputation at the Nobel Prize ceremony and again this reduces the reliability of the source to a historian.

> A historian would have to examine the source's attribution as there is no author of the citation for the award. Although the source does include factual content that King didn't lose faith in his methods that were so popular, the source's attribution decreases the validity of the source to a historian when questioning if King was the main reason for the success of the Civil Rights movement. Also the speech would not recognize other factors that were influences and it also doesn't have the reflection that a secondary source has.

> The source's usefulness is increased by how it supports my knowledge and understanding of how his beliefs brought him so much support during the 1950s and 1960s. His non-violent approach gathered mass support from not only African Americans but also the media as well which benefited greatly to King and the movement.

Again there is an attempt to judge the value of the source but this analysis is in isolation and is not linked to the particular enquiry about King's leadership or to the formation of any particular school of thought over the reasons of the success of the Civil Rights movement.

SOURCE 4

King's inspirational oratory and charisma made him the leading spokesman for black Americans in the years 1956–1965. His 'I have a dream speech' was the highlight of the March on Washington in 1963. His Birmingham campaign in the same year contributed to the passage of the Civil Rights Act of 1964 and his Selma campaign was vital to the passage of the Voting Rights Act in 1965.

[Extract from Chapter 7 in the book *Civil Rights and Race Relations in the USA 1850–2009* written by Vivienne Sanders.]

The source given here is not a primary source. It is an extract from a textbook written by a historian. As such it is not valid in the way it is used. If used it should be labelled as an extract and used as an example of a historian who reflects a particular school of thought — namely that King's leadership was fundamental to the success of the Civil Rights movement. This would have been much better placed earlier in the essay as an extract and the primary sources 1, 2 and 3 used to show how this kind of interpretation could have been reached.

Source 4 evidently supports the question being asked of was Martin Luther King's leadership the main reason for the success of the Civil Rights movement. It mentions all the factors that are considered to justify the reasoning behind King being considered as the most important factor. The source begins with backing up my own knowledge and understanding by declaring how his 'inspirational oratory and charisma' meant that he would be the lead spokesman for black Americans while fighting for the cause of black Americans. Also mentioned is King's 'I have a dream' speech which I have already mentioned as a backing towards King being the main reason for success. This shows just how essential his speech in Washington was for the progression of the Civil Rights movement. The whole source backs up all of the factors taken into thought when answering the widely debated question of Martin Luther King's leadership being the main reason for the success of the Civil Rights movement. The major turning points in the Civil Rights movement such as the passing of the Civil Rights Act and the Voting Rights Act are mentioned and are credited to King's contribution in fighting for these to be originally passed. Again this suggests that without King's leadership the idea for these legislations to be passed would never have happened. This backs up many historians' views of King being the main reason for success.

The evaluation comments on the extract are erroneous as it is used as a primary source. It is not — it is an interpretation. However, there is nothing wrong with the comments, if used to demonstrate a particular school of thought.

The source is written by Vivienne Sanders and is useful in my enquiry. Sanders has written many books on the race-related problems in America and specializes in this subject which adds great credibility to the source and increases its value to a historian. Again the source's value is increased as Sanders is a historian who would have hindsight on the matters spoken about and the book itself is focused making it more reliable and valid. Sanders is well educated and well respected and this also makes the source very reliable. The extract is from a chapter focused on Martin Luther King and because it is on the key figure in the question the validity of the source is increased also.

Such comments on the authorship of the extract are often seen in NEA work. These are spurious and formulaic and are not worthy of credit. Analysis of varying interpretations needs to be done in the context of different schools of thought about the issue and the veracity and range of the evidence base.

> However, whilst King's contribution and leadership towards the success of the movement cannot be denied, historians have identified other factors that could be equally as or more important than King's influence.

This is a simplistic statement which drifts by mentioning contribution, leadership and influence — which is it? — but it does hint at a balanced answer emerging. It also provides a clear bridge between two parts of the answer.

> During this horrid time of prejudice towards African Americans, Martin Luther King seemed to prevail as the key figure that looked to push the Civil Rights movement in the right direction. However, to many black Americans this was not the case. Some believed that his idea of peaceful protesting was taking them into a warzone and there are many cases of this where a protest turned sour when it was intended to be non-violent.
>
> There were also many significant figures that argue against the matter that King was the most important factor in the progression of black advancement in the 1950s and 1960s. Malcolm X is one of these figures considered to be more important due to his belief in black power — not just being equal to the white man but being superior and this is what appealed to rebellious black Americans in the North where King did not have as much of an influence.

The briefest of hints that there is another school of thought over this issue but it goes no further than that. There is no attempt to introduce the next source as support for another school of thought.

> **SOURCE 5**
>
> **No I'm not American. I'm one of the 22 million black people who are the victims of Americanism. One of the 22 million black people who are the victims of democracy — nothing but disguised hypocrisy. So I'm not standing here speaking to you as an American or a patriot or a flag-saluter or a flag-waver. No, I'm speaking as a victim of the American system. I see America through the eyes of the victim. I don't see any American dream: I see an American nightmare.**
>
> [Malcolm X, 'I have a nightmare' speech at the University of Ghana, May 13 1964]

This extract from Malcolm X's 'I have a nightmare' speech was a direct attack on Martin Luther King's 'I have a dream' speech. It challenges the ideology of the American Dream which King looked for in a hope to bring in key support from white Americans. Malcolm X targets the black working class in the ghettoes of the north where problems were different. King speaks as an American but Malcolm X believes he is a victim of the American system. The speech shows the rebellious side of the Civil Rights movement where Malcolm X is perceived as the key figure by many historians.

The statement is very bold and starts this way where Malcolm X says 'I'm not an American.' He is trying to appeal to the African Americans who feel victimised by the American white society who have mistreated them throughout their lives. He is not saying that he doesn't want to be an American but he is showing that right at this moment of time that black Americans are not classed as Americans due to the racial divide that originates from slavery in the south. Malcolm X uses the known power of America and turns it against them by saying that it is Americanism that is the reason that blacks have been mistreated. Malcolm X is trying to get his point across that throughout American history the minority in America has been a racial scapegoat and blamed for their own problems.

The speech which is an answer to Martin Luther King's 'I have a dream' speech goes on the whole belief of touching the lives of the white middle class and the patriotism of Americans, whereas Malcolm X speaks about not being 'a patriot or a flag-saluter' which would have offended white society in America and also King who had worked so hard to get this part of society onto the side of the Civil Rights movement. The powerful phrases that make up this speech show Malcolm X's goal and that peaceful protests weren't always the greatest choice because he helped the progression of equality or what Malcolm X would have hoped for which is to be superior unlike King.

The source questions the statement of King being the main reason for success as it shows just how great Malcolm X's methods of tackling racial prejudice were during the 1960s and this is shown by how his legacy still prevailed after his death in 1965 when the Black Panther movement took over his ideas in the late 1960s and 1970s.

The source's value to a historian is increased due to this matter as it shows that although Martin Luther King was a very strong factor in the success of the Civil Rights movement, there were other key figures that helped the Civil Rights movement to progress.

There is a lengthy attempt at evaluating the source from Malcolm X. However, the attempt at evaluation lacks any clear reference to the historical context or any link to an alternative interpretation of the issue. Indeed, it fails to identify anything specific about the author and his relationship with the Civil Rights movement.

In 1964 there was a landmark of the Civil Rights movement; it came from the man who was President of the United States, as Johnson passed the Civil Rights Act through Congress. It proved that progress was being made. Of all the different types of demonstrations that black leaders took it upon themselves to gain equality or go further, without the help of President Lyndon Johnson who took the role of President after the assassination of John F. Kennedy in 1963, passing of the Civil Rights Act and the Voting Rights Act could never have been possible. Both acts being passed showed great progression for the Civil Rights movement and the work that many leaders such as Martin Luther King and Malcolm X had been worthwhile.

A completed example

There is no attempt to link this paragraph to the preceding ones. It refers clearly to another key reason for the success of the Civil Rights movement — the support and involvement of senior US politicians. A linking phrase to this end would be of value.

> ### SOURCE 6
>
> **The 1964 Civil Rights Act prohibited discrimination on public places, furthered schools desegregation, gave the federal government the legal tools to end segregation in the south and established an Equal Employment Commission.**
>
> [Extract from Chapter 7 in the book *Civil Rights and Race Relations in the USA 1850– 2009* written by Vivienne Sanders.]

The source used here is not a primary source. It is taken from the same textbook as Source 4. Obviously it is also not valid in the way it is used. It is of little use, even if labelled as an extract, as it is not an interpretation, but a statement of fact in relation to the legislation of 1964. The candidate could have been advised to replace this as part of the Formal Review.

> Although Martin Luther King protested to get these bills passed through Congress without Johnson being President it could never have happened and it suggests that if there was another President then some of the laws passed would never have been possible. It was perfect timing that while Martin Luther King was doing his work, Johnson had become President to be able to support the views of equality for the Negro in America. Source 6 is extremely relevant as it disagrees with the statement that Martin Luther King was the main reason for success in the Civil Rights movement as the work of Presidents Kennedy and Johnson was instrumental. Without them Martin Luther King would have been going down a dead end in search of these laws.
>
> An argument against Johnson using this fight for African Americans as a way to gather votes from blacks is that after the Selma marches he started to really show that he cared by using quotes of Martin Luther King and his importance in the Civil Rights movement is undeniable.
>
> The source's value to a historian is shown in how it displays that without Johnson being President of America, these laws would never have been passed through Congress meaning that we might still be here today without these bills being passed if Johnson hadn't been in the right place at the right time.

The comment is erroneous in several ways, not least the descriptive nature of the writing and the fact that the source does not refer to Johnson at all.

There were many times that a Martin Luther King 'peaceful' and 'non-violent' march against racial discrimination turned violent. King always seemed to preach the methods of Gandhi, but many black Americans felt the real violence from the police and white Americans especially in the south. With no intention of fighting back apart from through preachers at local churches, marches and speeches, many African-Americans got injured when Americans fought back.

The Selma to Montgomery marches were three marches from March 7–25 with the last march taking place on March 21st. Selma and the marches on the Edmund Pettus Bridge showed how brutal the attacks on peaceful marches could get. Alabama state troopers and locals took matters into their own hands when Martin Luther King marched over the bridge to protest for the right to vote.

This does not seem to focus at all on the issue in the question. It seems a descriptive passage which is critical of King's methods.

SOURCE 7

Photo of the events at the Edmund Pettus Bridge in Selma, Montgomery on Sunday, 7th March

The photo shows State Troopers using tear gas as a force against protesters along with the use of batons. The protesters really had no chance against the use of brutal force without any attempt to fight back. Source 7 is from the first march which took place on the 7th March and the goal was to cross into Alabama and march to Montgomery and exercise their constitutional right to vote. The first march is now known as Bloody Sunday due to many demonstrators being injured from the brutality of the Alabama State Troopers. One of the organizers, Amelia Boynton, was so badly beaten by the enforcement that it created a national outcry as the media published a picture of her lying unconscious on the floor.

A completed example

Events spiralled from this march as once again violence came from white nationalist groups and James Reeb, a civil rights activist, was murdered on the night of the second march on March 9th. Around the country came many acts of civil disobedience due to the actions that took place on Bloody Sunday and the murder of James Reeb. These happenings back up my argument of how Martin Luther King's non-violent methods caused injuries and civil disobedience suggesting that his ideologies weren't always the main reason for the success during the Civil Rights movement.

The last statement is valid and would have been better used to introduce the photograph as displaying evidence which could help to formulate an interpretation of King's leadership as being less responsible for the success of the Civil Rights movement than other historians argue.

The usefulness of this source is reduced by how even though there was violence and scenes of disarray, from the events of Selma, Johnson passed the Voting Rights Act through Congress and it was another victory for the Civil Rights movement. It was a historic event as Johnson spoke on live TV demanding that Congress pass the Act and on March 17th two days after his speech the Voting Rights Bill was introduced in Congress. This shows again the importance of Johnson.

The source is useful in many ways as it shows the treatment that African Americans received in the south of America particularly and while King knew of this treatment he still attempted to protest without the fightback that Malcolm X and the Black Panthers took when violence came from the other side. While tear gas was being thrown and batons were being used to injure protestors, King's supporters could only run away and this was certainly a weakness for King's movement.

This is not an analysis of the source — there is no link with the forming of a school of history is apparent.

There is a suggestion amongst historians that without the long battles in the court against racial segregation led by the NAACP that the Civil Rights movement wouldn't have been as successful without the triumphs of historic cases such as *Brown v Board of Education*, *Little Rock High* or *James Meredith*.

As a final paragraph, this is weak. The conclusion needs to summarise the findings of the answer as a whole. There were hints throughout the answer regarding the role of King and the importance of other aspects such as Malcolm X, political support and the support of a wider social group in the USA, but these are not mentioned here. Rather the answer refers to some incidents that have not even been mentioned in the body of the work. This could have been done much better.

Applying the checklist

If the checklist on p. 57 is applied to the completed example, the evaluation might read as shown in Table 4.

Table 4 Applying the checklist to the sample answer

Checklist	Evaluation	Advice
Is the knowledge shown in the essay accurate?	To an extent. There are some minor errors. The biggest weakness is a failure to discuss the historical context which surrounds each source.	Briefly discuss the historical context which surrounds each source. For example, why was there a march on Washington in 1963? What was happening to provoke this demonstration?
Is the essay lucid and coherent?	The structure is basic but can be followed.	Try to link each paragraph to the previous one.
Does the essay address the question set?	A major weakness is the lack of an appropriate conclusion which answers the question.	Improve the conclusion — it is weak.
Does the essay show analysis and evaluation of a range of 6–8 primary/ contemporary sources?	No. There are five primary sources and two quotes from a history book presented as primary sources.	The range of primary sources is sound, but the two quotes from the history book need to be replaced by primary sources.
Does the essay evaluate the selected primary/ contemporary sources to test the validity of the interpretation contained in the question?	Sources are linked to the roles of King, Malcolm X and Johnson; the evaluation comments on the sources do vaguely attempt to comment on different interpretations, but this is done in a simplistic and formulaic manner.	In order to link the sources to the varying interpretations of the issue, it is important to move beyond occasional comments about 'value to a historian'. The test is to evaluate the sources and then judge whether they help strengthen or weaken an interpretation.
Does the essay focus the analysis of these sources on addressing how and why the interpretation may have been formed?	Not at all. The evaluation comments are largely general and lack reference to context or specific enquiry.	The evaluation of the sources needs to focus on how a historian would be able to use the material to formulate or support a particular view.
Is there a valid discussion in the essay of the historiography surrounding the issue in the question — that is, is there a sound understanding of the developing historical debate?	Not at all. This is another major weakness. Apart from comments such as 'value to a historian' there is no indication that this is an issue that has been debated among different schools of thought.	Make sure that the opening paragraphs clearly outline the debate among historians. Once this is set down the evaluation of the source material can be done in relation to this debate.

■ Submitting your essay

Now you should be in a position to submit your finished NEA. There are three essential items that must be submitted:

- your NEA — a 3,000–4,000-word essay giving an answer to the question that you have been set
- the authentication form — a signed acknowledgement from both you and your teacher that the work submitted is entirely your own work
- the review record — either formal or specific — where you identify the outcomes of the review undertaken with your teacher

Additionally, you can include your learner log if you have completed one — but it is not compulsory.

Presentation

- Remember that your NEA should be word-processed using a sensible font and font size, so that your answer is easy to read. Also use appropriate formatting, with headers, footers and margins of appropriate size.
- The question you are answering should appear at the top of the first page of your NEA. Make sure it is the exact question that has been approved by WJEC. Don't be tempted to tweak it a bit.
- Every page of your report should be numbered.
- Include your name and candidate number on each page — including the title page.
- Include a word count at the end of your work — but don't include sources, attributions, footnotes or the bibliography in this. The word count demonstrates your ability to be lucid and succinct.
- Make sure you have checked all spellings and grammar by proofreading and/or using appropriate software.
- Staple the pages of your work in order and present it in a plain envelope folder. Your school should be able to provide one of these.

What to avoid

- Don't submit your NEA in a ring binder file.
- Don't use plastic poly-pockets.
- There is no need for a contents page — this is not a project.
- There is no need to label and name separate sections within your NEA.
- There is no need to include rough notes and drafts — but retain these in case any doubt is raised about authenticity by your school or by WJEC.
- Don't include printouts or copies of research that you have undertaken — for example, from websites or copies of chapters from books.

Summary

- Don't forget to include the authentication form and the feedback form with your NEA.
- Present your work using the advice provided by WJEC — it makes NEAs easy to handle and consistent in appearance.
- There are several things to avoid — try to avoid them!

Appendix 1 Mark scheme

This is the mark scheme for the NEA, split into its three AOs. The criteria in the right-hand columns define the qualities that are expected to be seen in work for each AO. Applying this mark scheme to your work ensures that the marks awarded are consistent with those awarded for all learners studying WJEC GCE History.

Assessment objective 1		
Band 6	13–15 marks	The learner is able to effectively analyse and evaluate the key issues in relation to the set question. A focused, sustained and substantiated judgement is reached. The learner is able to demonstrate, organise and communicate accurate knowledge which shows clear understanding of the period studied. The learner is able to communicate clearly and fluently, using appropriate language and structure with a high degree of accuracy in a response which is coherent, lucid, concise and well-constructed.
Band 5	10–12 marks	The learner is able to clearly analyse and evaluate the key issues in relation to the set question. There is a clear attempt to reach a substantiated judgement which is supported. The learner is able to demonstrate and organise accurate and relevant historical knowledge of the period studied. The learner is able to communicate accurately and fluently using appropriate language and structure with a high degree of accuracy.
Band 4	7–9 marks	The learner is able to show understanding of the key issues demonstrating sound analysis and evaluation. A judgement is seen but lacks some support or substantiation. There is evidence of accurate deployment of knowledge and a good level of quality of written communication with a reasonable degree of accuracy.
Band 3	5–6 marks	The learner is able to show understanding through some analysis and evaluation of the key issues. There is an attempt to reach a judgement but it is not firmly supported and balanced. Some relevant knowledge is demonstrated and there is reasonable quality of written communication which conveys meaning clearly though there may be errors in spelling, punctuation and grammar.
Band 2	3–4 marks	The learner provides some relevant knowledge about the set question which is selected and deployed appropriately. There is an attempt to provide a judgement on the question set. There is reasonable quality of written communication which conveys meaning though there may be errors.
Band 1	1–2 marks	The learner provides limited knowledge about the issue. There is little attempt to provide a judgement on the question set. There is an attempt to convey meaning though there may be errors.
Award 0 marks for an irrelevant or inaccurate response.		

		Assessment objective 2
Band 6	13–15 marks	The learner shows clear understanding of the strengths and limitations of the selected sources. The sources will clearly be analysed and evaluated in the historical context of the set enquiry. The learner will make a sustained and developed attempt to utilise the sources to directly answer the particular question set.
Band 5	10–12 marks	The learner is able to show clear understanding by analysing and evaluating the selected sources in their historical context, including considering the strengths and limitations in terms of the particular enquiry. The learner deploys the sources appropriately to support the judgement reached about the particular enquiry.
Band 4	7–9 marks	The learner is able to analyse and evaluate the selected sources to develop a response which begins to discuss the strengths and weaknesses of the sources in the context of the particular enquiry. The learner also shows awareness of the wider historical context deploying the sources to support the judgement reached about the particular enquiry.
Band 3	5–6 marks	The learner is able to analyse and evaluate most of the selected sources to develop a response which begins to discuss their use in the context of the particular enquiry.
Band 2	3–4 marks	The learner begins to analyse and evaluate the selected sources to develop a response which attempts to comment on their use in the particular enquiry. The evaluation of the sources is largely mechanical and lacks context.
Band 1	1–2 marks	The candidate uses the sources for their content only. There is limited evidence of the use of a range of sources.
		Award 0 marks for an irrelevant response.

		Assessment objective 3
Band 6	26–30 marks	The learner is able to discuss the question set in the context of alternative interpretations. The learner is able to consider the validity of the interpretations in terms of the development of the historiographical context, and is able to demonstrate an understanding of how and why this issue has been interpreted in different ways. The learner is able to discuss why a particular historian or school of history would form an interpretation based on the evidence in the sources used.
Band 5	21–25 marks	The learner is able to discuss the question set in the context of alternative interpretations, and in particular discuss the work of different historians and/or schools of history to show an understanding of the development of the historical debate. The learner is able to analyse and explain the key issues in the question set when considering the interpretation in the question.
Band 4	16–20 marks	The learner is able to consider the question set in terms of the development of the historical debate that has taken place. There is some attempt to explain why different interpretations have been formed and consideration of a counter-argument to that presented in the question.
Band 3	11–15 marks	The learner is able to discuss the question set in the context of the development of the historical debate that has taken place. There is some attempt to explain why different interpretations have been formed.
Band 2	6–10 marks	The learner is able to show understanding of the question set. There is an attempt to reach a judgement about the set question but it is not firmly supported or balanced. The candidate's discussion of the interpretation is valid, with reference to alternative interpretations.
Band 1	1–5 marks	The learner attempts to discuss the interpretation by tending to agree or disagree with it. Any judgement reached is limited and unsupported.
		Award 0 marks for an irrelevant response.

Appendix 2 Self-assessment grids

Here is a series of self-assessment grids that you can use to check on aspects of your NEA.

Question setting	Yes	No
The topic in my question is recognisable or mainstream.		
My question reflects a clear historical debate about the named issue.		
My question contains an evaluative term that enables me to make a valid and supported judgement.		
The topic in my question allows me to access a sufficient range of primary sources.		
My question doesn't overlap with the content of the Depth Study I am studying.		

Writing an introduction	Yes	No
I can tell what the question is from reading my introduction.		
My introduction makes reference to different interpretations and/or the developing historical debate.		
My introduction refers to the primary evidence base.		
My introduction suggests an answer to the question set.		

For each primary source that you evaluate have you:	Yes	No
Identified the type of source?		
Summarised briefly the content of the source?		
Identified and commented on the credibility of the author/creator?		
Referred to the potential audience?		
Considered the historical context surrounding the source?		
Considered whether the source can be corroborated?		
Considered how the source could enable a particular interpretation to be supported?		

Appendix 2 Self-assessment grids

For each different interpretation that you discuss have you:	Yes	No
Identified the particular interpretation as belonging to a certain view or school of history?		
Discussed whether the historian is writing with a particular purpose?		
Outlined whether the interpretation is adequately supported by a range of appropriate primary source material?		
Decided, with reasons, whether this interpretation is more or less convincing than other interpretations of the same issue?		

Writing a conclusion	Yes	No
I can tell what the question is from my conclusion.		
I have not drifted into description in my conclusion.		
My conclusion refers to at least two different interpretations or schools of history.		
My conclusion refers to the evidence base for creating an interpretation.		
My conclusion clearly contains an answer to the question.		

Presentation	Yes	No
My essay is word processed.		
My essay contains 3,000–4,000 of my own words.		
I have provided a word count.		
I have clearly referenced both primary sources and any extracts used and inserted these into the essay.		
I have labelled each page of the response with a header which includes my centre number, my name and number.		
I have included both footnotes and a bibliography.		

A final check of my answer	Yes	No
Does my answer show accurate knowledge?		
Is my answer lucid and coherent?		
Does my answer address the question set?		
Have I analysed and evaluated a range of 6–8 primary/ contemporary sources?		
Have I evaluated my selected primary/contemporary sources in order to test the validity of the interpretation contained in the question?		
Have I analysed these sources in relation to how and why the interpretation may have been formed?		
Does my answer show a clear understanding of the developing historical debate over the issue?		

A

advice, general and specific   56–58
assessment objectives (AOs)   9–10
   mark scheme for   75–76
attitudes of historians   29
audience   29–30, 42, 43
author-date style of referencing   54–55
authorship of a source   41–42

B

background of historians   29
bands in the mark scheme   11–12
bibliographies   55

C

checklists
   applying to sample answer   73
   final checklist   60
   interpretation accuracy/validity   36
   learner log requirements   59
   primary sources   23, 49
   requirements for appropriate NEA question   8
   self-assessment grids   77–78
   writing introductions   24
clarifying interpretations   20–21
conclusions, writing   52–53, 78
contemporary sources   15 see also primary sources
content of primary source   40–41
context of historical events   28–29
credibility of sources, judging   37–39

D

date of a source, considering   43–44
Depth Study   7
'developing historical debate', meaning of   17

E

evaluative words and phrases, using   49
evidence
   availability of   30
   judging credibility of   37–39
example essay   61–72
extracts
   definition of   16
   from historians' works, using   34–36
   referencing   54–55

F

final checklist   60
fonts   54, 74
footnotes   55

H

hindsight and historical interpretation   31
historical concepts, identifying   19
historical debate, developing   27
'historiography'   6, 17

I

independent working   13–14, 18–19
information gathering   21–22
internet research   22
interpretations, historical   27
   examples of differing   31–32
   forming of different   35–36
   testing validity of   33–34
   using in your essay   32–33
introductions, writing   24–27, 77

J

judging credibility of sources   37–39

L

labelling of primary sources   39–40
learner logs   58–59

M

mark scheme   75–76
   applying   11
   meaning of bands   11–12
   understanding   10
material see also primary sources
   availability of   30
   secondary   15–17
   volume of   22
   ways of gathering   21–22

N

NEA (Non-Examination Assessment)   5–6

P

page numbering   54
perspective of a source   42

Index

planning   18–21
  planning chart, creating   20–21
  planning chart, updating   50
  understanding the question   19
  your time   18–19
presentation of NEA   54–55, 74, 78
primary sources   15
  authorship of   41–42
  content of   40–41
  date of   43–44
  evaluative words and phrases   49
  gathering a range of   22–23, 37
  historian using to support an interpretation   44–45
  integration into your NEA   46–48
  labelling   39–40
  perspective of   42
  pitfalls to avoid   40
  purpose of/reason created   42–43
  selecting credible   37–39
proofreading   54
purpose of a source   42–43

Q
questions for NEA   6–7
  choosing appropriate   7–8
  examples of   19, 31–32

R
range of sources, using   22–23
referencing   54–55
research for essay, conducting   21–23
resources
  online   22
  recording in learner log   58–59
reviewing your work   56–60

S
secondary material   15
  vs primary   16–17
self-assessment grids   77–78
source material *see also* primary sources
  defining   15–17
  secondary   15–17
specialisations of historians   30
Specific Advice Form   57–58
spell checking   54
student role in the NEA   14
style of essay   50–51
submission of essay   73–74
  presentation   74
  things to avoid   74
supervision, working without   14

T
teachers' role
  before start of NEA   13
  during NEA progress   14
  general advice from   56–58
time of historical events   28–29
time planning   18–19
topics and questions   6–7
  choosing appropriate question   7–8

V
validity of different historical interpretations,
  testing   33–34

W
websites
  listing in learner log   59
  verifying   22
word count/limit   5, 54
working independently   13–14